The Five Sisters

A Young Norman in the Second World War

The Five Sisters
A Young Norman in the Second World War

JEAN EUGENE HAVEL

VANTAGE PRESS
New York

This story is not a work of fiction. For the protection of some people, certain names and dates have been changed.

Cover design by Victor Mingovits
Vantage Press and the Vantage Press colophon
are registered trademarks of Vantage Press, Inc.

FIRST EDITION
All rights reserved, including the right of
reproduction in whole or in part in any form.
Copyright © 2011 by Jean Eugene Havel
Published by Vantage Press, Inc.
419 Park Ave. South, New York, NY 10016

Manufactured in the United States of America
ISBN: 978-0533-164714

Library of Congress Catalog Card No: 2011910803

0 9 8 7 6 5 4 3 2 1

CONTENTS

1	Senlis	1
2	Back Home	7
3	Years of Discretion	23
4	Crowded Years	33
5	Agneaux	45
6	The Funny War	55
7	Adapting	67
8	They Take Shelter in Our Houses	77
9	We Too Are Men	85
10	To Hold	95
11	Preface	105
12	A Cupboard Bottom	111
13	Hope	115
14	Last Days	127
15	Rescue Comes From the Sea (Old Norman Proverb)	133
16	The Five Sisters	145

PHOTOGRAPHS AND ILLUSTRATIONS

Jean in the arms of his grandmother	19
The MS Normandie	20
Le Havre in the thirties	21
Philip and Juliet with our mother in the Hellandes	22
Martial Havel in Hambye	31
Le Havre in the late forties	153
The Havel family house in Hambye	154

The Five Sisters
A Young Norman in the Second World War

1
Senlis

"You have visitors."

Astonished, I looked at the invigilator and at the messenger. I was seated in a study room with forty other nine-year-old boys. One month had followed another one, then another one, and so on. Who was still caring about me? I hesitated.

"Follow the beadle," ordered the invigilator.

I got up. We walked through old grey stones corridors, flinty playgrounds, and suddenly were in an open space. By an old house I discovered Taee and Theresa. I ran and we kissed one another. Then there was a moment of stillness. We were looking at one another, happy.

As always, my young aunts seemed beautiful to me; and they were truly beautiful.

"We were in Soissons. As it is not far from Senlis, we decided to come and visit you."

I did not ask them what they were doing in the north of France. And they did not ask me any question about my life in Senlis. We were feeling back in Le Havre, in our Normandy, by our always unsettled sky and our sea full of splendid ships.

I looked at the clear blue eyes and at the light hair of Taee, at the sparkling chestnut eyes and at the sandy hair of Theresa. I was feeling home with their soft manners. I asked them if Gabrielle and Vev were also with them.

"They are not. They are staying in Le Havre. We wished to see you."

"Why is Philip not with us?" I asked.

My brother, two years younger than I, was at the same boarding school, but we had been forbidden to meet each other.

"We have to part to meet Philip," indicated Taee.

When I left, I knew that it would be long before I would meet my aunts again. But I knew that they would continue to love me and my younger brother.

In early October our mother had bought for me and Philip a list of clothes provided by the boarding school, written India ink numbers on each of them, and brought them to a counter in Senlis where a woman was checking that nothing required was missing. She had lightly kissed Philip and me good-bye. A man had requested my brother to follow him, and another did the same to me.

I was proud of my outfit, as it was part of a uniform that, especially with my rigid cap, gave me the feeling of being a young soldier. There were so many men wearing military uniforms in this year 1938, and they all looked important.

The man I was following took me to a grayish playground where about forty or fifty boys of my age were parked, all standing and silent. Suddenly an order to form in a row of two-by-two was issued. We were led to a refectory; we sat, keeping silent. After the meal we formed again in a row of two-by-two and were directed to a large study room. We sat there for an hour, formed a row again, and moved to a large dormitory. The clothes and the shoes brought by the parents had been set at the head of each bed. An invigilator ordered us to get in our beds as fast as possible, "and in silence."

At one end of the dormitory was a line of taps and sinks. I went there with a glass, my toothbrush, some toothpaste, and a piece of soap. An invigilator, looking astonished, went to me and asked, "What are you doing here?"

It was obvious as I washed one of my legs. Having a feeling that I had to reply something, I said, "I wash myself!"

"Hurry up!" he was able to utter after a hesitation.

In the evening none of the boys were washing themselves, and they were not washing themselves too carefully in the morning. Every night a stench was growing from each bed, and up to the last night at the boarding school nothing was done to remedy this unpleasantness. I had to adapt.

After a few days, each of them spent under a dark, grayish sky, we started to hear every evening the sound of a horn. Not used to that, I asked one of the other boys what it was about.

"Some noblemen are hunting stags in the wood."

As we were hearing the sound of the horn evening after evening, it was making me sad that grown men were having their fun at killing.

Each day was similar to each day: walking in a row again and again, attending classes, sitting silently in a study room, eating silently, to be at play, and this stench in the dormitory.

Families were allowed to withdraw their sons or their nephews on Sundays. Not many were doing it. So on Saturdays, we had to write to our families. As we had to remit our letters in opened covers, we were quick to learn that it was advisable not to criticize. For some reason there were excellent adventure stories in the library. During the hour in the study room before our breakfast, I had a marvelous time reading.

A book can be a wonderful companion, more than ever when we are feeling forgotten. Senlis was the place to feel forgotten.

I did not understand all this silence imposed upon us by the invigilators. I was surprised to observe that in the playground my fellow students stayed isolated from one another. So one day I came near one of them, a tall, thin boy who seemed to be cold, and asked, "What is it here?"

His answer was bitter: "Here is a place where diplomats, travelers, parents who are quarrelling dump their children."

I knew that our parents were in none of these categories, but it was clear that Philip and I had been dumped.

Also adults did not seem happy in Senlis. For instance, there was a playwright who had success selling his work only to his students. Already diminished by his old age, he was supposed to teach us French and Latin. It was clear that it was not his preoccupation. He needed the admiration and the affection that society did not lavish upon him. This was something that we, his students, could provide to Mr. Moisy, as he was called. In the classroom we were touched by his shy smile when he was teaching us. We had no illusion about his credit in the school. But we were pleased to have such a relation with an adult.

One evening we got lectured about the alliance with Poland against Hitler. The following afternoon we attended a performance by a group of Poles. We had expected representatives of our allies to appear in military uniforms. They had come in fantasy outfits, which did not reassure us.

To get to the forest, we used to follow the walls built by the Romans at the time when they were colonizing Gaul. One day we found along these walls splendid soldiers in blue, white, and red, turbans on their heads, long swords hanging from their belts. They were Moroccan spahis and each had his own camel.

Our row was marching in front of them. We saluted them with our "Salam aleikum" and they answered us in Arabic with large smiles.

4

One day a student in our ranks asked: "Why are they not in khaki outfits?"

"They don't carry guns," noted another one.

"What is the use of camels in front of tanks?" asked a third one.

Suddenly, a voice uttered: "They are not for fighting Germans, but to crash French crowds!"

Things were different. But just like us they were the prisoners of a power. We did not stop saluting them all the months they camped by the Roman walls.

One morning, exploring around my playground, I discovered a gallery with a stone stairway going down to another playground. I got down a few steps and saw Philip, who had also seen me. We were so pleased to meet again, until an invigilator separated us. But later we could do it again with the same joy.

Czechoslovakia had an alliance with France. We children knew nothing about this country, but we learned that a quarter of its population was speaking German and that Hitler had occupied the areas where they were living. To our surprise, French leaders were doing nothing. To us, an alliance had to be respected; otherwise, we ourselves did not get respected. On September 29, 1938, an agreement occurred between France, the United Kingdom, Italy, and Germany in Munich: Germans would keep the territories they had seized, provided that more than half the people of these territories spoke German. Nobody was to make any verification. Germany could mobilize more and more soldiers and knew that we were afraid of her.

"Peace had been saved," repeated the grown-ups.

At Christmas, Philip and I were happy to meet again at the railway station. We took the same train, then the same subway line, and arrived together at the house of our parents. Philip talked chaff a little about some teachers and invigilators. But we did not speak much about our life in the boarding school. We had eaten alternatively its waterish lentils, its greasy potatoes, its mealy beans, and its overcooked macaronis; we had walked in silence through its corridors and playgrounds; we had sat in silence in its classrooms and its study rooms. We had escaped many punishments—I better than Philip, a victim of his sense of humor. We had felt alone and powerless for a long time. But we had added a few months to our ages, which gave hope to us.

It was a crowded house that we rediscovered. A generous and hardworking widow, Mrs. Lahr, was assisting our mother in the last month of her seventh pregnancy the best that she could. Our two young sisters and our two young brothers were giving them enough to do, and now Philip and I were back. Every day it was clear that it was not easy to take care of every child, keeping it clean and happy, along with shopping, cooking, feeding, and having the place tidy. Philip and I did our best for not adding too much to the burden. We gave a little help and stayed unobtrusive. Soon Philip spent much time around Mrs. Lahr, who had a special fondness for him. Our mother managed to prepare a Christmas day we all valued, with presents for all and an excellent lamb roast.

It became clear to me that I would not spend my Easter holidays in the house of our parents, among brothers and sisters I barely knew. It was not a new situation to me.

2
Back Home

"I don't need you anymore!"

I liked when Iren was taking me for a stroll in my pushcart. She was quite a tall, sweet woman, with black hair and black eyes and a reddish complexion. She was not rushing me and I had plenty of time to observe people and houses. She loved to visit stores. She simply parked me near a display and got inside the store. I looked at the goods and women stopped by me.

This time Iren had spent much time in a bazaar. She had got back late to our mother's house. And my mother was concerned by my security. It was decided to send me back to Le Havre.

I don't know how my parents had arrived at this decision. They had married in Le Havre. I was born there in the house of my grandmother, just the year after my grandfather had died from sickness. My father had graduated as a chemist a few years ago, but apparently there was no need for a chemist in Le Havre.

It is never easy to get a job in a French province. Many youth migrate to the Paris area where you found a mingling of Bretons, Corsicans, Lorrains, Burgundians, Aquitans, Normans, and others, along with people from the south or east of Europe and from Africa. The 1929 economic crisis had made jobs more difficult to get and to keep; many businesses were failing.

With luck, my father was at last to get hired by a manufacturer of green paint for the cars of the French railways and paints for artists. It was not certain if artists would continue to buy paint, but the French government could always print banknotes to pay for keeping its railway cars in good order. The manufacturer was located among many others in a suburb called Montreuil-sous-bois. There was neither a mountain nor a wood, only cheap houses. Our parents had moved not far from the factory and rented the best of the cheap houses they could find.

The salary my father was paid every month was probably too mediocre to continue hiring a nurse for me. My grandmother had offered to take care of me for as long as circumstances necessitated.

It is said that the earliest memories we remember are from our third year. I am not certain about that, as I still remember Iren and the pushcart she used to take me for a stroll. I have another vivid memory of a scene that occurred when I was a little more than two and a half years old:

It was a dark spring day in Montreuil-sous-bois. There was a crib in the middle of a large grey room. In an armchair by the spacious bed of my parents my mother was seated. She offered her white right breast to a tiny baby girl. My aunts Taee and Gabrielle were waiting to make me move to Le Havre. I did not wish to follow them as long as my mother would not kiss me good-bye. Alas, she was staring at her baby, motionless. I was going to spend some time in Le Havre, and I wanted a sign of affection before leaving. But she looked only to her baby. My aunts were getting impatient.

"Jean, come!"

At last I left. My mother had not even given a look at me. I was sad. My aunts were pleased to have me with them, and I found myself examining them carefully, as I was feeling that now they would be my anchors.

I had been born in the house of my grandmother, and I had visited it a number of times later. I was feeling home in it. And I was fond of my grandmother and her children.

She was a small person, spoke little, devoted to her family and to her enterprise inherited from her husband, the "Ateliers Doré," with a sense of social responsibility. She looked at people full in the face from her dark eyes. She kept in a coil her black hair, never cut by a hairdresser, so long that if it was not arranged it would reach the ground. She used some discreet perfumes and was always clad in black dresses, sometimes with a shawl.

Her first task in the morning was to go to a center where volunteers helped young mothers with their babies. She herself had given birth to eight daughters and two sons. A manager and her two sons helped her with the Ateliers Doré. Now and then one of them came to discuss with her in the wide library full of leather-bound books. Most of the morning and the afternoon my grandmother was at the Ateliers.

Aged thirteen to the early twenties, Theresa (the youngest daughter), Vev, Taee, and Gabrielle were living in the large house, busy with their studies, taking care of themselves. Gabrielle was working as a shorthand typist. In her thirties, still living in the house, was also Lalen, one of the two eldest twin children. Her sister Looloo was married and already had two children, but few could distinguish between them. Lalen seemed to live apart in an isolated existence.

Lunch and diner were presided over by my grandmother. Sometimes she or one of my aunts brought fresh herrings from the harbor. Meals were the responsibility of the cook. All my aunts had to do was to lay the cloth. Children were not supposed to speak during meals unless asked to. From time to time my grandmother made a few comments about ships expected to arrive, some with cargos for the Ateliers, others of which the wooden parts had been the work of the Ateliers and, as such, were like a second family.

After lunch my grandmother was enjoying her coffee in the library. She drank not just any coffee, but an excellent one imported to Le Havre ("Not for children," I was told), read a newspaper, and relaxed with some crosswords. Then, as in the morning, Alexander, the chauffeur, drove her to the Ateliers, unless there was a meeting at the chamber of commerce, where ignorant or greedy officials too often made life hard for manufacturers, traders, and ship owners, as well as for the city and the harbor.

In the evening my grandmother sat in an armchair in her bedroom, relaxing with some knitting, reading a newspaper, or doing nothing—just enjoying having her family around her. I loved to stretch on her deep carpets.

One of these dark days when we hear the thunder, she commented, "Little Jesus is playing at bowls." I wondered how I could join him and play at bowls too. Time to time, my grandmother was absent. There was a hesitation in the routines, but never from the staff.

Each morning one or two of my aunts came into the red room where my bed was to tell me it was time to get up. One dressed me and took care of my elegance. Then she told me to follow her to the dining room, where my cup was the last one on the table. After finishing my hot chocolate and my little loaf, she let me do what I wished. And what I wished was simply to follow my aunt, chat a little with her and observe her, or to sneak to the drawing room, lay under the white grand piano, and listen to Taee play. She could play for hours and I never tired from listening Chopin's polonaises, which made me full of heroic dreams.

When Taee was playing, she never spoke. When she stopped she walked graciously toward one of the doors, opened it, and said, "Jean, come on." Then she vanished. Or, on a nice day, she took me to the garden and let me explore there. I could see on the opposite side of the garden the garage, and over it Alexander's apartment. He had children, but I was not supposed to speak with anyone from the staff.

Most of the time I found myself alone in the hall, not knowing what to do. The whole main floor seemed empty: the library, the dining room, the pantry, the cloakroom, just like the drawing room. After some waiting, coming downstairs appeared Vev, a woman of a light brownish complexion, chestnut hair, and kind, brown eyes. Always she had a proposal. When it was not rainy, we would go to the Francis the First Boulevard and turn left toward the Clemenceau Boulevard along the sea. The first years we did not walk very far. But after several visits I wished to get on the dike which parted the waters. Later, when we started to walk up to the dike, Vev never took the direction of the sea, but turned back home. As I did not wish to hurt her, I quickly joined her.

At other times Vev opened a hidden door under the stairway. There was a little room full of toys. I wished to take them all out. But Vev did not allow me to and I had to surrender to her smile and determination. Little by little the time went by, until it was lunch.

After the meal, I used to follow my grandmother to the library where she was having her coffee. I sat on a large bench and played with bright tokens of different colors.

From time to time, Looloo asked her younger sisters to take care of her children for an afternoon or a day or two. Martine, a fair girl of my age, and Sylvia, two years younger with hazel eyes, showed to be good company to me. When the weather was fair, Taee and Vev took the three of us to the Clemenceau Boulevard for a stroll.

Later, when we became stronger, our aunts started to take us towards the Sugar Loaf. For a time, climbing the stairway was too much for us, especially for Theresa when she was pushing Sylvia's cart. But one day came when we were able to get to the top. I had the feeling of having grown up. I had made a few steps here and there only to ensure that I reached the plateau of the Sugar Loaf.

This high monument had the shape of precisely a sugar loaf, the sort women in the past crushed with a bottle for the use of their families. It was all white, raised on the cliff, and could be seen from far away on the sea. It has helped navigation since time immemorial. Beside it is a chapel where sailors and fishermen who have escaped peril at sea hang miniature boats and other objects in thanks to Mary.

The view from the Sugar Loaf is a wonder. Among bushes of gorse, we could see the ships coming and going on the sea, the harbor with its dikes and its cranes, a part of the city. We the children became fond of the stroll to the Sugar Loaf, though our aunts found it hard to push the cart. Going there became a frequent walk. Now and then Taee pointed out to us the three smokestacks of the MS Normandie, arriving to Le Havre from New York or going back with her two thousand passengers.

In the chapel you could also see, engraved in gold letters, marble slabs expressing thanks for a rescue or candles telling of a recent drama. So quiet and beautiful under the sun, so generous to fishermen, the way to the whole world, the sea can at times become quite terrible.

Back home each child was given a glass of milk and a slice of bread with some jam on it "to wait for the dinner." In fact, the walk made each of us pretty quiet. Before the meal our aunts put all of us together in the warm water of a large bathtub. It was another effect of the walk that we did not splash much.

One day Taee and Vev were replaced for an instant by Lalen. We were seated at the bottom of the bathtub when Martine got up in front of me. Something seemed to be missing from her body. "You don't have a cock?"

Lalen jumped on her feet and ran out from the bathroom. Martine, seated again, seemed not to have paid attention to my words. Lalen reappeared, red and animated.

"We cannot have them any longer together in the bathtub!"

Taee washed, rinsed, and dried me. When I had put on my pajamas, she led me to the corridor and we walked a few steps.

"Jean, I am going to tell you a story. God made a man, then he started to make a woman and discovered that he had not enough cord. So girls are different from boys."

Taee's story amazed me. It would be fun to tell it again to Martine, thought I. I did not take the matter seriously, but henceforth I was going to bathe alone.

Taee noted that I did not enjoy my bath the same. A few days later, when I was in the water, she offered me five plastic ducks, each of a different color, and showed me that when I would fasten little camphor balls to the ducks they would move on the water. I did it; the ducks moved; I found them boring. I definitely preferred my cousins.

A few years later, when we had learned how to read, I spent much good time with my cousins, as they had become insatiable card players and no adult objected.

In the meantime, we children had discovered that Vev was a fascinating storyteller. When she was seated on a sofa in the hall, we immediately joined her and asked her for some story. But we had to persuade her. Then one child sat by her, the others at her feet.

"There was once upon a time . . . " Vev started.

She knew admirably the old fairy tales: Little Red Riding Hood, Tufted Riquet, The Donkey Skin, The Cat with Boots, Cinderella, Tom Thumb, Sleeping Beauty . . . She knew how to make us understand easily. And she always concluded in the traditional fashion:

"They were very happy and had many children."

She could repeat two or three times this sentence, which made us children feel important. But Vev never discussed a story. We stayed seated around her, dreaming. Only after a good while did Vev get up and go.

When Gabrielle instead of her sisters took care of me, was it on weekends, as she was employed as a shorthand typist? The routine was not much different.

Gabrielle was the tallest of the sisters, but also probably the shiest of them. She had nice brown eyes and her hair was of a chestnut color. Around her left wrist was a gold chain given to her by her father. Her clothes, elegant but never gaudy, translated her shyness.

When she came in the morning to the red room where I slept, she told me to follow her to her own bedroom and climb up on her large bed. The time I stood there, she clad me and told me nice words.

After my hot chocolate and my little loaf, we were out. She wore good walking shoes. Because of her stature, she was in no need of high heels. Her direction was not that of the sea. She liked to arrive at a public square. Often she went to the Lafayette stores. There we stopped by the windows and my aunt studied carefully the new apparels and the new shoes offered to the feminine public.

Then we went in. Gabrielle examined different presentations. Soon a girl or two were showing her pieces of fabric. It took time. I tried to direct my attention to the activity of the personnel and to the customers. After a while, a girl measured and cut some fabric for my aunt. She paid and we went.

Some time later Vev and Taee found it convenient to take me to the same stores to buy some fabric for themselves. In the afternoon, in a room of the second floor of my grandmother's house, my aunts cut their material according to patterns to make new dresses for themselves. The price of the fabric was moderate; they assembled them on a sewing machine, and soon they were happy that they could be clad the same as the most fashionable women. In the street I found my aunts magnificent, and I was proud to see how beautiful they were.

I had noted an attractive pastry shop with many cakes on the way back home from the stores. My aunts refused to get tempted. They were acting as if the pastry shop did not exist. In fact, after a lunch, Taee told me in the corridor when nobody was around, "You stop eating when you are still a little hungry."

I was not yet ready for appreciating such a philosophy.

It was understood that all the children of my grandmother, their husbands, wives, and children had to take their summer holidays at Les Hellandes. It was a huge, four-floor brick mansion that my deceased grandfather had built at about twenty kilometers from Le Havre.

My uncle Francis drove my four young aunts and myself to the castle, and then drove back to bring his wife and his children. My grandmother appeared at meal time. The gardener had decorated the hall with white mums, which diffused a fragrance all over the ground floor.

At first, children enjoyed the place: they were many and relatively free. Along a walk on the right side of the castle, a donkey was waiting for us with a small carriage. The most aged of us boarded the carriage; the animal pulled it smoothly; we went to the end of the walk, near a road, and the donkey took us back. It had done its work for the day, and whatever we children were doing it refused any other task.

There were the hens, white Leghorns, in an enclosure on the left side of the mansion, near a pond full of frogs and surrounded by a fence hidden among capucines with orange flowers. With Vev it was magical to collect the eggs laid in special boxes. The gardener told stories of foxes, but we were too young to get interested.

We could visit the two Norman cows in a field behind the castle; they provided the daily milk for my grandmother and her family all through the year. But these big animals were too quiet to be of much interest to us.

Suddenly the adults had decided to take pictures. Each parent assembled his offspring, found proper spots, and snapped away.

After that, for a while, we did not know what to do until meal call. In the large dining room there was a magnificent opportunity for playing at hide-and-seek under the tables, among the legs of the adults.

When he was in Le Havre or in Les Hellandes, my father was always hungry because of poor digestion. Our mother tried to victual him with bananas, but in the country it was difficult. My father stated to our mother that each child had to meet both of his families. Plainly it meant that he would take me on a Saturday to Laval to meet my other grandparents, leave me with them for a week, and then come back the next Saturday to pick me up.

French railways do not go directly across the country. To get from one city to another, you first get to Paris and then take another train. Gabriel volunteered to take care of me between Le Havre and Paris.

In summer, my grandparents on my father's side moved to their family house in Hambye, in lower Normandy. Our mother found that she preferred to spend summers with the parents of her husband: their house was large, as was their garden, and they used only a small part of the property, allowing our mother to do whatever she liked. In these circumstances, our mother prepared two trunks of clothes and shoes and other necessities, hired another maid, Mrs. Lahr, staying in Montreuil-sous-bois, assembled her children, and moved to Hambye. Little by little she introduced electricity, gas cooking, and other modern improvements in the old house. Time to time our father had a short visit.

In those times, trains were not as fast as today and stopped in many stations. I learned to observe the landscape and the activity in the stations.

It was clear that my father's parents were pleased to see their grandchildren, but it was clear too that they were tired. An old maid was helping them and moaned when she had also to do work for Philip and me.

Our paternal grandmother woke up late in the morning. At their winter house in Laval, her maid took us to her bedroom and provided her with a large jug of warm water and a sponge. My grandmother moved slowly, but was still enjoying caring for her grandchildren.

More or less fixed, we went down for a bolus of pap. By his fireplace, our grandfather was reading in Latin, the language of learned people in his time, in a book by Horatius, this plant lover who taught us to take care of the moment, or in the Ecclesiastes in his old, big Bible . . . Or our grandfather was doing nothing, watching us.

After having taken some food in her kitchen, our grandmother took me (if I was alone), or Philip and me (if we were both staying in their house) for a stroll. I remember her pace, still quite agile, and her brown cotton stockings falling down on her legs. Usually we went to a pastry shop in one of the towers of the old wall around the city. Our grandmother invited us to eat some meringues. Sugar was not allowed in my grandfather's house, as it was sold by slave owners. The meringues were a secret shared with Grandma. Then we went through the old streets of Laval to a beautiful public square dominating the valley of the river, La Perrine. Grandma sat for a while on a bench, giving us plenty of time to explore the surroundings.

After lunch, Philip and I, or I alone, spent time in a room on the second floor and played with carefully carved, small wooden toys. Later, in my bed, I enjoyed the flames in the fireplace and their play in the darkness until I fell asleep.

One day, when I was still six years old, our father told me that his mother had died. I did not cry. It was a void. Something would never come back. I was pleased I had met her.

Another day in Montreuil-sous-bois, I heard from the radio that Britain had authorized Germany to get as many submarines as her, but only a third of her tonnage in surface ships. I mentioned that to my father who was shaving himself with all the necessary care. He did not reply.

Back in Le Havre, Taee and Theresa took me and Philip for a stroll. We did not go through the usual streets. Soon they were becoming narrow. An increasing noise of striking metal became unbearable. Theresa hesitated to push further the cart transporting Philip. Taee was watching. I looked. Despite my stature, I could see on two dry docks many men quickly completing unfinished hulls painted orange.

Taee and Theresa considered them for a while. Then Taee explained, "They are making four submarines. When the hulls are completed, they will be sent to Saint-Nazaire."

The noise was too much for our comfort. We turned back and walked towards the Clemenceau Boulevard. There all seemed quiet and peaceful; the waves of the sea seemed to roll in the same motion as at low tide.

Near the house of his grandmother Marie Doré, Jean, three weeks old, in her arms in 1928.

The MS *Normandie* used to carry up to 2,200 passengers between Le Havre, New York, and Southampton at a speed of up to 32.64 knots. 373.73 meters long, she was 36.40 meters wide. She was operated by a crew of 1,300 men and women. Launched on October 20, 1932 in Penhoët stocks for the "Compagnie Générale Transatlantique," she was burned down in New York Harbor on February 9, 1942.

In the thirties, the house of Marie Doré was on 75 Francis the 1st Boulevard, in Le Havre. *Edition CM, Le Havre.*

Our mother with her second and third children, Philip and Juliet, in the park of the Hellandes, near Le Havre.

3

Years of Discretion

Philip and I had hoped that he would stay longer in Le Havre this time. In general, his presence made it easier for our aunts to care for us, as we were doing things together.

The dike was still forbidden to us. It would be only years later that we would walk with joy on this road between a quiet dock and a never-exhausted sea banging its waves against a wall put by humans. Philip walked quickly, then paused, then watched the captured water, then climbed up on the wall of protection to see the wild motions of the sea, his short chestnut hair in the wind and his big brown eyes in his face animated by the challenge.

We got sick at the same time. We started by the measles. We found it funny to see our bodies all red. We wondered if sicknesses made our bodies green, blue, yellow, or another color. Our aunts Taee and Vev had diplomas from the Red Cross, and consequently treated us well and carefully. We were supposed to stay quiet under our bedclothes. But the truth is that as soon as we could and when we were alone, we danced on our beds.

As soon as we got healed from the measles, our bodies got covered with pimples. To us the phenomenon was amazing and interesting. Our aunts continued to treat us with the same care. At the Red Cross, their devotion and their kindness certainly made them many friends among the patients. But at the time it was not a consideration for Philip and me. There were days when the chicken pox made us tired. But soon again we were dancing on our beds. Our aunts were not blind to our behavior. When our health became good again, it did not take long to have us returned to our parents.

Now each day in Le Havre Alexander was driving me to a little school. We were children of the same age in one room that was occupied, in large part, by a grand piano. Two women were trying to teach us something and made us relax with jumping games in an adjoined room. It was a quiet, sunny place. At the end, I had covered pages with straight strokes and could write them without making too many ink stains with a steel pen, which I had to dip into a black inkwell.

It was a time of low skies. Fishermen continued to go out on the open sea, but were quick to get back to shelter. One evening Vev told me that she and I would get up early the next morning to accompany my grandmother. At said time she woke me up, and Alexander drove the three of us to the fishing harbor. The sky was grey and it could rain at any time. A few slim women were selling fish on stalls of wood covered with fir branches. Time to time a big basket appeared at the edge of the wharf, full of fresh fish. I gave a look downward. It was deep. A small boat with three men on board, in blue, wearing old caps on their head, was moving up and down along the wall on yellowish-brown water.

My grandmother was choosing two or three fishes among black-stripped blue herrings. The woman who was selling them put them quickly in a newspaper and Alexander drove us back. I gave a quick look to the kitchen as my grandmother was hurrying to help with the babies.

The following day the weather did not improve. I was told that fishermen did not dare to leave the harbor, though some did on a small motorboat.

In the afternoon after school, Taee, Vev, and Theresa asked me to accompany them. They had concerned faces. We started with our usual walk along the sea. It looked like boiling water, with ripples going up and down. My aunts told me that the small fishing boat had not come back. Soon we could see it far away, appearing and disappearing on the water. A group of thin women with black dresses and coils of black hair was standing up on the strand, still.

"We must stay at a distance," said Vev, "as they need their privacy."

The boat reappeared. We could distinguish the profiles of the fishermen. Then it disappeared for moments which seemed long. Suddenly, we heard a detonation.

"A cable with a harpoon had been sent to them," explained Taee.

But we could not see anymore the little boat. After a while, which seemed too long, we saw it again and we heard a second detonation. Did they get the cable?

We never saw the boat again. Silent, we went back home.

The year went by. There was a wedding. But what can a six-year-old boy do attending a wedding? Our mother and her four other children were going to spend the summer in Hambye. It had been decided that I would join them.

To get from Le Havre to Hambye, which took much time by train, Alexander drove Taee, Vev, and me through Normandy and stopped the car at Hôtel des Bains in Granville, at a few kilometers from Hambye. We had been through Caen, along the big old fortress of Duke William, but we had not paid much attention to it. The Ateliers Doré had a manufacturer there too, but we did not go by it. We marveled at the beauty of the coast with its green vegetation, the blond gold of its sands, and the multiple changing colors of the sea under a nice sky where two or three small clouds were still hanging.

The hotel lays at a breach among the rocks towards the beach of Granville. We got a two bedroom on the third floor and a cot was added for me. On the side of the room was another one, very small, with windows opening onto the sea. I felt that this was especially for children and spent much time there, contemplating the water and the sky and their changing, multiple colors at the different times of the day.

In this beginning of the summer the three of us went down through the rocks. A farmer had already driven the parents of my father and me to Granville in a horse carriage. We had not spent much time as it seemed that rain would happen soon; together we had eaten some cold chicken and some bread before hurrying back to Hambye. It had also happened that, while in Hambye, our mother had sent my brothers and sisters and me by bus to the same beach in the care of her maid. The weather had been pleasant and we fished for sole and gathered crabs and shells, which the maid had cooked for us all. Nights had been a little difficult, as we were sharing with the maid her only bed; large, doubtless, but a bit narrow for six people in the only room of the small house she rented.

The fine golden sand of Granville was a pleasant discovery for Taee and Vev, used to the stones of the Le Havre seashore. With joy and enthusiasm, they rushed their pace, and I had to follow them at their speed until they stopped in front of layers of rocks covered of black mussels and some other shells and some brown seaweed. I wished to collect some mussels for our meal, but my aunts told me that we would eat in a restaurant. So we just followed some of the rivulets of the low tide, enjoyed our time, and went to the restaurant of the casino by our hotel, where a cook really knew how to prepare a delicious hake covered in cream. In the afternoon we were back to the beach; much of it had already disappeared under a tide higher than a house. We then started to stroll in the streets, nearly always climbing up as Granville had been first built on a high, rocky peninsula. Another day we spent our time in the little harbor. Then we took a bus to Hambye, where our mother was waiting for us.

Our mother and her two sisters had so much to talk about, and it was such pleasure to be together, that they decided Taee and Vev would come back to Hambye. Our mother did not have a hesitation telling them that, at her in-laws' house, Taee and Vev would have to fix their beds, prepare their breakfasts, clean up behind them, peel carrots and potatoes, and generally help.

I had already found my tasks: to convey water from the well, to bring wood for the fires, to help in the kitchen garden and in the flower garden, to put in order what I had used, and to keep an eye on my younger brothers and sisters. I was proud to help with house and garden work, but felt that having to watch over my brothers and sisters was building a distance between them and me.

Our mother was respectful of everyone, and everyone could see her working. When she needed help, it was clear that she appreciated it and was only asking for sharing tasks. At times she was laughing with people and making friends with them.

The end of the day had a moment of anxiety. When we had blown away the flame of our lamp or of our candle, we knew that we had to wait until the end of the night to see light again. In an old house in the country, there are plenty of noises inside and around, enough to make you afraid at times. We had to learn not to care and just sleep.

Taee and Vev left after a few days. Again I was invited by some of the neighboring farmers. I was especially pleased to go with Alice when she was taking care of the cows. We used to stop at a fountain in a sunken road; Alice was careful not to disturb the plants growing around and above, and loaded her donkey with pails of water. Then we continued in the sunken road, surrounded by trees, blackberry bushes, ferns, and other plants, to the fields and arrived at one where the cows were waiting for us. Each one had a name and we knew its individuality, and each cow was showing gratitude for every caress. Alice watered and milked each one. The pails which had transported water were now full of foaming, tepid milk.

Getting back to the farm, Alice was careful not to hurt anything alive. She had tuberculosis like many people of the time. She was a slim blonde girl, always clad in a checked blue apron and shod in wooden clogs. Her sickness seemed to give her access to an invisible world.

We all loved Tuesdays, as in town they were market days. Farmers gave us a lift in their horse carriages. The main street was full of people and stalls. There were open boxes with screaming pink piglets. There were cages of hens or ducks. People walked slowly and stopped to speak with merchants, family, or friends. The notary made sure not to miss any business that might be around. Shops were full of people.

Angela, the sister of my grandma, had a house always open on Tuesdays. The family of my father was visiting her and sat in a circle of chairs, drinking her cider or her white wine, eating her biscuits, exchanging news and jokes, putting large baskets full of goods in a corner of the room. My mother was always sending me to the baker to buy eight pound loaves, too many for me at a time; farmers' wives bought twenty-four pound loaves. They did not carry them, as their horses stopped at the baker's door.

One day followed another in the warmth of the summer. No one helped us children to wash ourselves. We knew that we had to look clean and well-combed to get access to large slices of bread, toasted before the flames of the fireplace. This toasting was irregular, with spots of carbonization; the maid buttered them and, as they were still hot, part of the butter melted. We got butter all over our fingers, but found these slices delicious.

Time to time, merchants stopped near the house. One was coming in a horse carriage and bought rags and animal skins. Another arrived in a little lorry from Granville with fresh fish. Others offering goods such as haberdashery did not visit every week.

On Tuesdays the mailman waited for people in the town main street. On other days he had to visit every address for the letters he was carrying. Late in the morning he would bring letters to our paternal grandfather. He used to stop his bike by the gate of the flower garden and walk to the house door. He delivered the letters and waited. Our grandfather had a glass and a bottle of red wine on a shelf at the entrance. He filled up the glass with some red wine and the mailman took some time drinking before leaving. It was not his first glass, neither his last, as people offered him some wine wherever he went. People also said that he had some difficulty cycling at the end of his round.

The custom was to give a drink to every public employee sent from Paris who did something for you. Policemen were treated with a special generosity, and not with cider or red wine, but with cider brandy. It was believed that after a few months they had become a little more human and understanding.

Before getting to Hambye, I was playing in the house of my grandmother in Le Havre, trying to stop Theresa getting through an entrance. Taee had broken off our game.

"Jean," she said, "you know that you will soon reach your years of discretion?"

"I don't understand what you mean."

"There is a time when you are no longer a small child," explained my aunt. "You start to understand many things."

"Sure I do," I said.

"It means that you are reaching the years of discretion. You will have to go to school every day. It will no longer be possible to keep you here."

"Where shall I go?" I asked.

"Your parents will tell you."

I got afraid for a while, then returned to my play with Theresa. But something had been broken. I was no longer feeling safe.

A few days later, as I was admiring the superb pictures of a book about immigration into the Roman Empire, I stopped my aunt Taee.

"I am already going to school. Am I going to the same school as Martine?"

My cousin was about the same age as myself.

"No, she is a girl. Girls don't go to the same school as boys. They are not learning the same things: cooking, sewing, embroidery, music."

"I like music."

"Girls' education is not as serious as boys'. You are a boy."

And my aunt left.

Now I had spent two months in the house of my paternal grandfather, under the care of our mother. The day came when he left, followed by his maid; then the day when our summer maid left. The next day, one of the neighboring farmers helped our mother, with her baby, move her two trunks into his horse carriage, then my four brothers and sisters and me. For two and a half hours I enjoyed looking at the landscape, the people, and the animals from the height of the carriage. After an eighteen kilometers ride we arrived in Villedieu, where we boarded a train to Paris.

Martial Havel, Jean's paternal grandfather, and a maid in the kitchen of the family house at La Cave, Hambye, between Saint-Lô and Granville, in lower Normandie.

4
Crowded Years

I had never realized how little the house of our parents in Montreuil-sous-bois was until the moment when I was added to its population. They decided that their youngest child would share their bedroom. It allowed our two sisters to occupy another bedroom and for Philip and me to use the third one. The washroom was minuscule and it was established that our father, as the breadwinner, would have priority to use it.

Mrs. Lahr in her small kitchen, with the baby by her, had been happy to meet Philip again. He had stayed longer than any of the other children in the baby chair, as he had been born with clubfoot that necessitated surgery and plastering. She was now back to her routine, with one more person: me.

Soon school and youth club gave relief to our parents. Our mother was afraid to entrust others to help her youngest children. Maybe she did not have the money? Happily Mrs. Lahr was a devoted and hardworking person.

I had the good luck to be registered in a small private institution, the school of Mademoiselle Lemouton. She and three other women were teaching, boys and girls together, the twelve grades of the official French primary and secondary education. The number of students was small, and part of the teaching was through books only. Older students were helping younger ones. The atmosphere was conducive to learning quickly.

Getting to school was a walk of a little more than a half hour. I enjoyed the freedom it gave me. I was alone without any grownup to watch me and direct me. The streets were just houses after houses, with few shops. But it was this feeling of being by myself. . . . Often I walked in the company of another boy by the name of Gilbert, as free as me.

When returning, I got a glass of milk and a slice of bread with some butter and jam from Mrs. Lahr. When it was cold, we children had to get to our bedrooms until we would be called for dinner, a plate of soup and a sweet. When the temperature was clement we waited in a minuscule yard, separated from the children in the street by bars.

There was no school on Thursdays. Philip and I attended a club, where we played games outside with other boys. A walk to a wood and some movie viewing agreeably completed our day, for the relaxation of our parents. One time I saw Philip aggressed in the street of our way back home; I ran and jumped over a tall fellow. It took no time for him to punch me with such blows that Philip was standing on his feet before me. But the fellow had fled, and this episode had strengthened our brotherly solidarity.

On Sunday mornings, our father went to an open market with a big bag. Often one or two of my brothers and sisters and I accompanied him. The merchants advertised loudly their vegetables, their fruits, their eggs, their cheeses, their meats, and everything they could sell. At an entrance to the subway, a group of Communists proposed their daily newspaper, also in a strong voice: "Ask for, read, spread out *L'Humanité*, the paper of the Central Committee of the Communist Party!"

We loved to be offered samples by the merchants: a banana, a tomato, some cheese, some candy. And it is so good to eat a warm tomato and some cheese when browsing through a market!

One sunny Sunday afternoon, I saw our mother adjusting a hat on her head before leaving. I asked her, "Why are the Japanese in China? What are they doing?"

Our mother showed surprise at my question, looked at me, and left. But on the third of October 1935, the Italians were entering into Ethiopia. I did not speak about this event to our parents. It seemed now to me that they had enough to be concerned with their family and my father's work. For them, an immediate preoccupation was about what to do with their offspring during the next school holidays.

For these Christmas holidays, they did not get any relief. Our mother was brave enough to offer each of us nice presents and to the whole family an excellent meal of roast lamb and green beans, followed by a custard immediately devoured.

On the end of an afternoon in January, back from school, I found my grandmother visiting our mother. Our mother was no longer going to Le Havre or to Les Hellandes. Both were seated in the drawing room. As usual, my grandmother was clad in black. She was on the point of departure to go and visit her sister Martha in Paris, whose husband had been gassed during the First World War and depended fully upon her. She gave me with a smile her kind of shy kiss. I was pleased to have met her again.

Already in November our parents had had another baby, who was now occupying the crib in their bedroom. Our grandmother had admired this new grandson of hers. A consequence of her visit was that one week before Easter Aunt Gabrielle was again in Montreuil-sous-bois. She took me right away to the Saint-Lazare Station, from where most of the trains to Normandy depart. In the compartment she called me two or three times her favorite utterance: "My golden treasure."

She was the only person, aside Iren many years ago, to call me by terms of endearment. Our father was used to insult me and I tried to understand why; when he took me and my younger brothers and sisters for a walk, he always went too fast, pretending that it was for our own good. I was feeling happy to be back in the big house on 75, Francis the First Boulevard. Nothing seemed to have changed, except me. I no longer needed anyone to care about myself. As before, aunts and cousins were around. On Easter morning my aunts brought to me, as I was still in bed, a big chocolate egg. At lunch there were small yellow plush chickens on the white tablecloth.

Later in the afternoon I was looking down into the boulevard from the red room window. Theresa joined me. She was fifteen years old now. Then Taee and Vev.

"Will the Italians take Ethiopia?" I asked.

"In the past, Menelik expelled them," said Theresa.

"Will Haile Selassie do it again?" I uttered.

Taee and Vev entered into a discussion. We were the four of us around the window. I felt that there would be a big war and that that window would no longer exist. I shook myself to get this vision off. I just wished to enjoy what was good in this moment. I went back to Montreuil-sous-bois with Aunt Gabrielle, to the school of Mademoiselle Lemouton and to the youth club. Later I was in Hambye with our mother and my brothers and Aunt Gabrielle gave me a beautifully illustrated book telling the story of a poorly treated boy, Adam, who had gotten away and found love and fortune. My sisters and my aunts visited. Then we were back to Montreuil-sous-bois; I was again at Mademoiselle Lemouton's school and at the youth club.

On the seventh of March 1936, my father was warming up a small pan water for shaving himself. I mentioned to him, "The Germans are getting into the Rhineland."

Did my father hear me? I was not too concerned. The Rhineland being part of Germany, I knew that some day German soldiers would be back there.

Aunt Gabriel took me again to Le Havre for Easter holidays. From time to time my grandmother had visited our mother. Spring became a strange time.

In Montreuil-sous-bois, low-salary people were in a new mood. Communists were bragging about Stalin who, according to them, would soon control the "capitalists."

On May 3, 1936, the Socialists and the Communists, allied in a "People's Front," won the elections. On May 5, the Italians took Addis Ababa, the capital city of Ethiopia. Our parents stayed mute about these events. Left and right, each felt stronger.

On the May 25, there were strikes in every French manufacturing plant. There was a strike in the paint manufacturer of our father. His boss requested that he stay nearly all the time there to protect the premises. So our father came back home at the end of each day for a short rest and spent each night at the manufacture. Every day he was more tired; his eyes were becoming small and red. Our mother was concerned.

"Our workers are not very young and they are good people," he kept repeating to her.

On June 4, the Socialist leader Léon Blum was appointed prime minister. Everyone had the feeling that change was coming. The pressure increased among the striking wage-earners. On June 8, they were all given better salaries and strikes ended.

On June 20, Parliament enacted a statute granting every salaried people fifteen days of paid holidays per year. The next day it reduced the forty-eight-hour working day to forty.

The right was dumbfounded and afraid. On the left, wage-earners had the feeling of being now treated like people; the joy was immense, militants proud. One day the extreme right would try to take revenge, but the left was not thinking about that.

On July 17, the Spanish military in the Rif in Morocco rebelled. The following day it was imitated in a number of cities in Spain. In Madrid the Socialist government started to distribute weapons to civilians. On July 25, in Burgos, General Franco took the lead of the revolt. Léon Blum, the French prime minister, had to be prudent so that the Civil War in Spain did not run over into France.

In July, as usual, our mother had decided to leave Montreuil-sous-bois and to get back to Hambye. Our parents believed that the family would be more secure in Normandy.

For a few days our aunts visited again. Our mother was pleased to see her young sisters, and all of them spent much time seated in the flower garden, not far from the door, helping with the vegetables for the meals, knitting, chatting.

It happened that Albert, the father of Alice, lost an arm in an agricultural machine. His wife and their two daughters attempted to continue the work on the farm for a few months. But it was too much for them and the whole family had to leave. On what would they make a living? Charity?

Immediately another family came to replace them. Land was in high demand. It was also a time when a young couple did not need more than experience and a reputation for being hardworking to rent a farm of ten or twelve hectares. Soon they had a dozen milk cows, a strong mare, pigs, hens, ducks, a cat, and a dog.

René and Germaine Burnouf, the new farmers, had a large family. They were not lazy and knew how to cultivate and take care of the animals. From time to time Philip, our younger sister Juliet, and I were invited to go to the fields when they were taking care of their cows. But no one replaced Alice. The Burnoufs took excellent care of their fields; they did not save the plants around the fountains or form ceilings over the lanes. However, something was telling me that the fairies were not gone. They had lived for so many hundred years in this country, and the landscape would not always be one of strenuous exploitation.

Our father had added the task of painting fences to what he requested from Philip and me. We still had time to play together with lead soldiers in the small fir woods our paternal grandfather had planted many years ago, and where we had plenty of space to deploy our "armies."

Quite rarely our mother authorized us to play with the daughters of another farmer couple. They were of the same age as us. They were thin girls with very blue eyes and pale complexions. Our favorite occupation was to play the merchant and the customers. The truth is that the whole time allowed to us was used to build the store and find the "goods." Our father considered that country youth were "sane."

Our mother had a big swing installed near the house. She was the one to use it the most, but we were pleased to use it alone or to push one or the other of our younger brothers and sisters.

A couple of times the same maid who had taken us children by bus to Granville the previous summer did it again. The place was no longer the same. Well-off holidayers formed a separate group near the casino, away from people using for the first time their paid holidays. So we walked further, to the beautiful wide beach of Donville. Our maid kept silent. We know that her friend was a communist. So many people were.

We had spent our nights the same in the large bed in the small house rented by our maid in Granville. Six people was definitely too many. We had to awaken many times.

At breakfast time we were joined by our maid's friend, a little man with dark hair and a red complexion. He did not speak much. We had only learned that he was working in a Michelin tire factory. Our maid detected a bottle of red wine and he was drinking slowly from his glass, eating the same good tepid bread as us, with an abundant layer of butter.

One time, when he left, he said to our maid, "Soon we shall be in power. You will get better wages and you will get good holidays!"

Journalists explained that Japanese were trying to colonize China, the same as the Italians were Ethiopia. At the end of July they had taken Beijing, the capital city. But the Chinese resisted. It took three months for the Japanese to penetrate into Shanghai. They killed an enormous amount of civilians. The pictures in the newspapers were tragic. But people did not comment on them.

On November 9, the Japanese had taken this big harbor. Other cities were falling into their hands: Guangtong, Hankou, Nanking . . . many people died. The Chinese were heroically defending their country. A vast and diverse territory with few modern roads and railway tracks gave them an advantage. And they were so many people.

In January our mother had another birth. A few days later she was standing up in the corridor of the house in Montreuil-sous-bois, considering her new line in a black coat, pleased with herself. She saw me and asked how she looked. I was not used to being consulted by our parents, and she was our mother.

"Fine, mother."

She turned on herself and added: "When he was helping me for the delivery, I asked Doctor Tridon to sterilize me."

I did not understand. So I kept silent.

"Do not tell," she said.

A few weeks later our parents and four of my younger brothers and sisters and I were seated around the table of the dining room. Plenty of sun was getting into the room and again attractive food was on our plates. Our parents were silent. All a sudden our mother addressed our father: "You don't like babies."

Our father kept silent and we finished our meal without a word, as middle-class children in those times were not supposed to address grown-ups.

War was my concern. It seemed to me that neither in Hambye nor in Montreuil-solis-bois did people understand that the events in Asia had a relation with those in Spain and in Ethiopia. The interest was in the Spanish Civil War and the foreign participations in it; the weapons sent by Germany, Italy, and the Soviet Union; and the "International Brigades."

My aunts and I were waiting for my grandmother around her table in Le Havre. She was unusually late on this April 26, 1937. When she appeared she looked tense.

"In Spain, German planes have bombed the little town of Guernica," she indicated. "There were no soldiers there, only civilians. They have killed thousands of people."

Taee and Vev asked immediately for details. We were stunned. Germans were Europeans and they could do that?

We took our meal in silence. My grandmother was the first to leave, probably to pray. She knew about what had happened between 1914 and 1918. The books used in school did not tell too much about that.

The following morning my aunts had started a discussion in the washroom and continued it in the red bedroom where I was. Vev believed that the conflict was limited to Spain and that most probably the Germans would not commit a similar crime. The authors of it had to be punished, and certainly German authorities would look at that.

Taee did not believe it. She even compared it with some atrocities of the First World War, that no court of justice had ever dealt with. To her, because of the Germans, the Italians, the Soviets, and the "International Brigades" of volunteers coming from all over the world into Spain, and because of the same social conflicts through Europe, war would spread. She observed that the successes of German and Italian tanks in the Spanish war were giving Germany and Italy an incentive for assaulting other countries. Theresa remained silent.

We all agreed that in any case no civilized country would tolerate war crimes such as the one perpetrated in Guernica.

Again Taee, Vev, Theresa, the cousins and I climbed up to the Sugar Loaf. We saw through a light haze the three smokestacks of the MS Normandie and her impressive silhouette of three hundred seventy-three meters. She was still winning the "Blue Ribbon" for her speed of thirty-two knots for her return trips to New York. But in our dangerous times we did not care much.

Gabrielle and Theresa went with me to other places this time. We walked around the small docks of the ancient harbor, but my preference was to get where the tugboats were moored. Liners need at least one mile for stopping, and have difficulty turning around inside a harbor. It was marvelous to see three of these small ships pulling and pushing the huge liners to put them in position for disembarkment, then the big ships to sail again on the seas.

I wished to see more of Le Havre and asked my aunts to have Alexander take us to different places. Gabrielle answered that in difficult times for workers, we had to show them respect and therefore walk.

My mother took again all her children to Hambye. In China, the Japanese were trying to move inside the country from the coasts where they had the support of their navy.

We were back to Montreuil-sous-bois in October 1937. Our parents decided that Philip and I should attend a "true" boys' school. Our mother bought us uniforms with brown velvet breeches, not offering us much protection against the cold of the winter. The fashion of the "good" schools was to show the skin of our thighs and our knees. I really liked to wear a cap with a hard, bright peak; to me, it gave my garb a certain military look. Mrs. Lahr commented quickly that that was a stupid idea.

The so-called "true" boys' school happened to be an agreeable surprise. Philip and I had been told that we were in need of a harsh discipline to make "men" out of us. It was certainly strange not to see any women or girls in this school. What we found were teachers as humane and devoted as the female teachers of Mademoiselle Lemouton's school.

That winter our aunts visited. Taee came a couple of times. She brought me silhouettes of soldiers to cut out and Gabrielle a toy bicycle. Vev visited too.

A few days before Easter, our father took me one grey morning to Saint-Lazare Station and bought a train ticket for me.

"You are nine years old. You are grown up enough to travel alone in train."

He led me to the convoy and I boarded alone one of the cars. There was no one in my compartment. When I saw a couple of hours later the walls of Le Havre station, I started to feel safe. Nobody was waiting for me in the station. Outside I discovered one of my grandmother's cars. Alexander opened a door for me. Soon I was ringing at the door on Francis the First Boulevard. Gabrielle opened the door for me. She apologized for not having been able to take care of me this time. But we were just happy to be together again, nephew and aunt.

On March 13, 1938, I had informed our father, who was shaving himself, that the radio had announced the entrance of Germans in Austria. I did not receive an answer. Children were supposed to speak only when addressed by grown-up. In Le Havre, my grandmother considered this news as serious. To them, war was going to erupt. Theresa was asked by the French military intelligence if she would like to get back among the family, which had received her, in order to perfect her German in Silesia. Our grandmother became afraid, but Theresa refused. The plan was not intelligent, and the position would have been too dangerous.

The holidays in Hambye seemed surreal. Our paternal grandfather continued pruning in his garden; our mother took care of everything; we the children went a couple of times to Donville, on the same beach near Granville, to its marvelous sand; the aunts visited again. . . .

With us children getting older, the house in Montreuil-sous-bois was becoming more crowded. A decision was made to send Philip and me to a stern boarding school in Senlis.

5
Agneaux

Philip and I had definitely left Senlis in July 1938. It was strange to be again in our family. Mrs. Lahr made the change easier for Philip: he was welcome by her in the kitchen, and she took him two or three times on weekends to enjoy some happenings.

We barely knew the other five younger children of our mother, and it was clear that they looked upon us with some jealousy and shyness. I was looking for the moment when we would be back in Hambye, as there were there many resources which did not exist in Montreuil-sous-bois.

One morning our mother sent me to the baker. It was not far from home, about three hundred meters. Everywhere, on all the sidewalks, sat Spanish soldiers in uniforms. None was carrying any weapon. I managed to move among them. There was not a gesture, not a word from them. They seemed stunned. They were probably men who had defended the elected Spanish government. The people of Montreuil-sous-bois sided with it, and it was probably the reason why they were here. But what was so terrible had made all these young men seem as if they were dead?

A need for togetherness and security pervaded the whole family. Our parents decided that only our father would get back to Montreuil-sous-bois and that the remainder would stay in our Normandy. There was plenty of room in the house of the father of our father in Hambye. Food and fuel were abundant in the country. Aunts, uncles, cousins, friends announced their visit. So it was not two trunks, but three that our mother prepared before our departure from Montreuil-sous-bois: shoes and clothes for the winter, tools and other objects we could need during a long stay, some valuables.

However, our parents decided that as I was a boy of ten years old I could be a challenge to our mother, and that for the discipline of her children and the good of my education it was better to send me to another boarding school. There was one at one walking day away from Hambye, in Agneaux.

This summer the big family house in Hambye was crowded. There was work for everyone, but it was a pleasant time. We had plenty of conversations; we had long walks all over a beautiful country hilly and green; my grandfather had a large library; we were of course spending time listening news on radio; and I had great enjoyment playing cards with my cousins Martine, Sylvie, and Arlette.

Arlette was vivacious and funny; she was also always looking for comfortable places away from grownups. Time to time, she made jokes and we laughed with her.

She was not going to become one of these young women impressed by their beauty. She was a very normal brunette. But what she had was humor, intelligence, and a strong epicurism. You had a feeling that life with her was something good to eat on every day.

Martine, a slender, fair girl, was agreeable too. But her intelligence was more towards books and philosophy.

Sylvie, a brunette, had an appearance of distinction and spoke little; but she had humor and was a good partner.

It was easy to get to my new boarding school in Agneaux. One of the buses which stopped in front of the house took me to Saint-Lô, and I walked a couple of kilometers. The boarding school was in the country. There were no walls around. It was one big building and a few smaller ones around a large park. At first, the way of living, classes, organization, and food were similar to what I had known in Senlis. But soon it was different. The people were our people, with the same ways, more interested in good relations and achievement than in strict discipline. Something else appeared too. As valid men were busy in their specialties or in military functions—these last ones seemed to have much to do with cafés—the male personnel of the boarding-school were older men or men of diminished capacity. Women who were employed by the boarding school served in traditional occupations in the kitchen, in cleaning or in mending. So, the very first day of our formal education, after our first lessons, we were requested to go to the park. It had been occupied by British troops, and to keep them busy their sergeants had them dig trenches below the high building of the boarding school. No one saw any use for these holes. The administration of the boarding school asked us to fill them. As it was grownup-man work, we did our best, and in a couple of days it was done. The old gardeners were pleased that soon they could seed grass on the earth we had shoveled.

The fences around the property were only for the cows we could see around. As said, no walls separated us from the landscape. Apples were still falling down from their branches and leaves had the darker green of season's end.

The equipment was the same as in Senlis. In washrooms there was a primitive hole at the level of the ground. But in the dormitory no one interfered when I washed myself before going to bed.

In the morning we were served either soup or coffee and milk or chocolate and milk to drink with buttered bread, according to how much our parents were paying. It was the first time in my life that I started my day with soup, and soon I had my mother pay enough so I could get chocolate and milk.

Outside classrooms and study rooms, no one forbade us from speaking. That we "fell in" was not a concern for the personnel. In fact, we soon discovered that these men were not able to impose a discipline upon us.

There was an exception. It was the mathematics teacher. I don't know if he ever followed a program during the school year. His way was to ask us to do different operations on different numbers and to whisper to him the results of our calculations; then he announced who among us had been right. He was a former boxer, and his body was still full of muscles. We had the feeling that he was still ready to use his fists and none of us wished to test the speed of his reactions.

Monsieur Bonnet was in charge of teaching us Latin and French literature. A diminutive man in brown lounge suits, he started normally his classes. But silently he started to cry; after a while he apologized and left the classroom. Two students helped him to go to the sick-ward.

Monsieur Bonnet did not last three weeks. The boarding school never found a proper replacement for him. Different men who barely know Latin or French literature attempted to teach us; we probably knew more than them. At the end, the time for Latin and French literature became a reading time and the library of the boarding school became a wonderful resource.

Plenty of learned women could have been the right teachers for us. But we were in a "male" institution. Many times I had heard Taee complain that the education of girls was sabotaged, that intelligent and able women who had graduated, despite obstacles, had difficulty getting adequate positions and were not equally rewarded. She was especially scandalized that a woman who had gotten married had lost her legal capacity to administer her belongings—and, at that time, generous fathers were wise giving to their daughters at wedding time jewels and gold coins in case of difficulty.

But these matters were not discussed in Agneaux. As we had been told that it was not healthy to smoke, we had got an urge to experiment this "vice."

During one of these afternoons when it seemed that we would not get a teacher for matters on the program, Gilles, a thin boy with black curly hair, confided to us that he wished to smoke and that the moment seemed perfect to him to go to Saint-Lô with no one to see us. Soon we were five boys all determined to smoke as soon as possible.

Leaving the premises was easy. We just jumped into a field where a few cows gave us a look, and we moved from field to field along the road to the town in a way that no one would see us. We arrived to a few narrow small streets and found a little old tobacconist. We checked that we had enough money. The question was which brand of cigarettes to buy. We studied the window. There were elegant red and gold packages marked "High Life." They seemed to answer exactly our purpose. We got into the store and asked for a package of "High Life." An old, small woman took one and held it out to Gilles.

"Do you need matches?"

"Yes, please."

We had forgotten about matches.

Now we were ready to commit the forbidden. Our concern was not to be seen. A corner of an old street seemed exactly what we were looking for. Gilles opened the package. Then he showed to each of us the twenty cigarettes neatly set. We had a smell of them. Gilles took one, then the tall Claude, and each of us.

Now each of us had a cigarette in his mouth. Gilles lighted a match and soon we had all a burning cigarette between our lips. But we had never smoked.

"You inhale the smoke, then you release it," said one of us.

Immediately, we were all inhaling and releasing. We were tasting the cigarettes and rejecting a blue smoke.

"Now," said another one, "you don't have to hurry so much. You have to get the smoke into your lungs."

We took more time for each puff. We coughed a little, some more than others.

"This is good," said one.

"Yes, this is good," answered a second one.

"Maybe we should not smoke all the cigarettes at a time," observed Gilles. "We have to get back and not get caught because we would have smoked too much."

We finished our cigarettes, then we blew in the face of one another.

"No, I don't smell anything," we were saying.

We had not understood that none of us could detect the smell of the tobacco or the sent of the smoke, as each of us had smoked.

We took the same way in reverse to get back to the playground we had left a moment ago. And then we joined the other students to get into a classroom. No one paid any attention to our odor.

The music teacher came. We sat down at our desks. He took a little instrument from his pocket and got a few sounds from it. When he felt contented, he declared, "Today, we still have to polish the 'Marseillaise' verses for the youth. Repeat after me:

Bien moins jaloux de leur survivre
Que de partager leurs cerceuils,
Nous aurons le sublime orgueil
De les venger ou de les suivre!

("Much less eager to outlive our elders

Than to share their coffins

We shall get the sublime pride

Of avenging them or of following them!")

We were eleven years old. All these songs they were teaching us were speaking of death. We were getting a bitter taste in our mouths. How could these older men dare to teach us that we had a duty to die? They were well alive. Many years later I still had nightmares that I had to run toward German machine guns, singing their patriotic songs, and get killed.

I spent my Christmas holidays with our mother, my brothers, and my sisters in Hambye. Our father visited for two days.

Philip was happy not going back to a boarding school. Since I had left to Agneaux, he was attending the school of the borough. Every morning he walked along the road with our sisters and a large group of other children from the area. Because many were young, they moved slowly. In fact, the landscape with its animals and its plants provided them with many opportunities to observe or to stop. The farmers' wives, taking care of their cows, had a look on the children. For our mother, she felt more secure having Philip with her daughters. The sociability of Philip made him many friends among the children. He was where he belonged.

Our mother was making the house more comfortable. The previous year, she had had installed a big wood stove containing a provision of hot water. Now a sheet of metal was protecting it from the drafts in the big kitchen chimney. Our paternal grandfather had permitted it, as it was still possible by removing it to cook a full lamb or half a pig on a fire. The largest bedroom had been transformed into a warm dormitory. There was a bed for each of the seven children and a broad one for our parents; there was a washroom corner; and there was a wood stove with a long slanting pipe for its smoke. The pipe retained much of the heat which, otherwise, would have disappeared with a traditional vertical stack.

Our mother had also made sure that every tree no longer healthy on her father-in-law's property had been cut and made into logs. On a side of the kitchen garden, a nurseryman had planted for her five-year-old apple trees, which would soon yield good, big fruits.

We did not get many toys, as our mother had no transport to a city except the bus between Granville and Saint-Lô early in the morning and late in the evening. Yes, she had a maid as always, but she could not entrust the present one—too young—with her children. However, the food from the farms around and from our kitchen garden was the best freshness could offer.

The second term in Agneaux was just lost time academically. The boarding school as said, did not consider female teachers, so it could not get the competent personnel it needed.

At Easter I used a combination of trains that took me to Le Havre. The invasion of the remainder of Czechoslovakia by Hitler on March 15, 1939, had definitely convinced my grandmother and her family that war was unavoidable. It would be terrible for Le Havre and its inhabitants, she was saying.

When my aunts, my cousins, and I had climbed up to the Sugar Loaf, we saw in the sun the MS Queen Elizabeth—the brand new ship of the Cunard, built by John Brown's yard on the Clyde—sailing back to Southampton.

"We shall not see her again for a long time," noted Taee.

"Why?" asked Vev.

"She will transport soldiers," explained Taee.

I had not yet seen her sister, the MS Queen Mary, which was going to win the "Blue Ribbon" at a speed of 31 knots in August. Soon she too (and the MS Normandie, we believed) would transport soldiers and material from North America. We did not think that speed would be an asset to escape from German submarines.

We discussed for a while about the fate of the MS Normandie. We knew she was in good hands, the "Compagnie Générale Transatlantique." I was never going to see the MS Queen Mary.

The second day of my arrival in Le Havre, Theresa had started a conversation with me in the red bedroom and shown surprise that I had not heard in Agneaux or in Hambye about many events. However, the people of these places were not living outside time. They were only interested in the circumstances upon which they could act.

Taee had not stopped to play with passion the music of Chopin on the grand piano. But now Theresa, like her, was not letting me ignore the news from the world. Their family was a constant exchange center, never commentating more than necessary so as to leave room for other pieces of information to reach you. News was coming from everywhere, and not only from the media. Sources were as varied as the personnel of the house, of the castle, of the Ateliers Doré, the chamber of commerce, the baby center, the Red Cross, the bankers, the traders, the merchants, the customers, the family at large, Theresa's school, and the captains of the ships the Ateliers Doré had worked for. In this way, my grandmother knew the best prices, the best merchandise, the best rates of exchange, which ship or which merchant would need the Ateliers Doré, which danger was menacing. This is how you make a fortune and help people.

Theresa told me that Mussolini had invaded Albania. We did not know much about Albania. But we strongly believed that it was not an Italian war. Mussolini had conquered Ethiopia and Albania, but it was with a people interested only in peace.

My grandmother and my aunts had a special concern for Spain, on a border of France, where so much cruelty was displayed. It came into their evening meal conversation, among the furniture of heavy black wood where light disappeared. The resistance against the military push of Franco was going underground. Toledo and many other cities and villages had fallen into ruins; many inhabitants had been killed, tortured, raped, or maimed. The dictator had been clever enough to get the help of the tanks and planes of Hitler and Mussolini, happy to make power demonstrations, without becoming their ally. On the contrary, he showed much friendship towards the Roman Catholic Church, a foe of communism. My grandmother was of the opinion that the correct way of treating employees was through good salaries and good working conditions.

Aunts, cousins, and I walked through different parts of Le Havre not too far from the house. Something was happening. We did not know what. One thing was certain: all the merchants, all the entrepreneurs, all the sailors, all the fishermen, all the women were feeling the scent of war. Preparations had started. Stocks had gone smaller. Things could not stay the way they used to be.

I managed to get back to Hambye through different trains, and from Hambye to Agneaux with the bus. In Agneaux schooling was no longer a concern. The institution was dormant. Students did not wait for the end of the term to get back to their families.

In Hambye everyone was cultivating more than usual. Special attention had been given to potatoes, as they can replace bread when there is not enough of it, and are difficult to steal when they are in the soil. Some fields would be turned from grass to wheat and buckwheat. Fewer newborn animals were declared to the authorities, and veterinarians were the accomplices of the farmers. Family and friends were visiting in larger numbers and for longer periods of time. In this way I met again my aunt Gabrielle, who I had not seen for a while and who was now employed in a small town far from the coast.

People in Hambye did not believe the news from Czechoslovakia. They refused to think that Germans were practicing in this country a kind of colonization resulting in the deaths of enormous numbers of victims.

On September 1, 1939, understanding that he had no one to fear, Hitler invaded Poland. I still remembered the Polish singers in Senlis and wondered what kind of resistance they could have presented. Newspapers published pictures of brave Polish horsemen charging vainly against German tanks. The media spoke about horrible massacres. People did not know what to do with such information.

6

The Funny War

On September 3, 1939, at the end of a beautiful afternoon, Philip and I were in our bedroom in Hambye. Our father opened the door, did a few steps, stopped, hesitated, and then uttered, "France and England have declared war against Germany."

We knew that it was the thing to do. Our father left.

On the tenth, Canada too entered into the war against Hitler. Other countries such as Australia were doing the same.

At this time there was an abundance of soldiers in France. Hitler was busy in Poland. It was the time to attack him. But nothing was happening. One day; two days; three days . . . Women were knitting sweaters and socks. French and British troops did not invade Germany and did not rescue the Poles. Nobody understood.

No, it was not the way we boys were used to acting.

Sixteen days were thus spent carelessly. The radio spoke of terrible slaughters in Poland. All of a sudden, as Germans had now conquered half of Poland, Soviet troops rushed to occupy the other half, recuperating a portion of the former empire of the tsars.

We could not understand why our leaders had declared war to Germany. What kind of people were they? Something had to happen now because of them. If it was true that Germans had killed more than six millions Poles, what would happen to the inhabitants of the Western European countries when they would invade them? Some people were getting afraid.

It was often reported that some men looking like officials, managers, or even military officers explained that a "new order" was necessary, that blue collar workers had to be put to "work" and "disciplined," that a democracy which had granted paid holidays to employees had to be replaced by a "more serious" political regime which would build speedways and get rid of Jews, gypsies, negroes, and all colored people, like the regimes giving so much strength to Germany and Italy . . .

The radio was warning us to pay attention to the "Third Column." Were these leaders of society the "Third Column?" To us, children, this "Third Column" appeared so mysterious that it sounded exciting.

Grown-ups were circulating stories. According to one, the French government had not completed along the Belgian border a powerful line of fortifications. Called the "Maginot Line," it was being built along the Rhine, on the German border. Was the meaning of this unfinished work that we would never attack? Was it an invitation to the Germans to step in through Belgium?

According to another one, in order not to make soldiers jealous, the French government had granted one tank to each infantry regiment. No tank unit had been organized. No one knew how to use one tank in coordination with an infantry regiment. It was told that staff officers knew only about the tactics of the First World War (1914-1918) and of colonial wars, but had not read a little book, published several years ago, translated into diverse languages, written by still-young officer Charles de Gaulle, *Au fil de l'épée*. This work explained that tanks had to be used in large units, the same as cavalry in the ancient wars. Germans had attentively studied this work and were building many tanks. They had organized large armored mobile units. And they were discussing tank tactics for their next offensives.

On November 30, 1939, we learned that Soviet Union had attacked Finland. Immediately Sweden had sent twenty-five airplanes, weapons, and materiel to Finland. Eight thousand Swedes enlisted to help the Finnish army as volunteers. France, Britain, other countries were also sending materiel and food to Finland. The Soviet army was in a poor condition and was fighting awkwardly. Moscow had been more concerned with expanding revolutions than preparing war.

The British navy had not waited to start cleaning the seas of German warships. On our radio sets we followed the hunt of the battleship Admiral Graf von Spee from the north to the south of the Atlantic Ocean. Her speed gave her an advantage, but on December 17, getting short of gas, her crew exhausted, the Admiral Graf von Spee entered the wide and powerful Rio de la Plata, between Argentina and Uruguay, and scuttled herself.

After Christmas 1939, we heard about the Finnish victory at Suomussalmi on December 30. It was not credible. Moscow sent better troops, which invaded Carelia in March 1940. At a peace treaty, Finland gave up to the Soviet Union areas allowing them to strengthen their defense of the city of Leningrad. We were happily surprised that the Soviet Union had respected the independence of Finland.

War was approaching. On April 9, 1940, the Germans invaded Denmark and disembarked on many points of the one thousand seven hundred kilometers of the Norwegian coast, but not always easily. In the south, Norwegian guns in the Oslo fjord sank the German battleship Blücher. In the north, British ships sank a few German ships and routed others in the area of Narvik, the transit harbor for Swedish iron ore.

They disembarked British and French troops, which, with the help of Norwegian troops, recaptured Narvik. Alas, order came to the British and the French to get to France to resist another German invasion. The Norwegians fought until June 7; then in both Norway and Denmark the task of continuing the fight went to a clandestine resistance.

The Norwegian royal family and Parliament were able to reach Britain on some of the four thousand motor ships of Norway, the largest and the most modern fleet of motor ships in the world at the time. A few thousand Jews escaped to Sweden or to Britain. On the other hand, the Germans had brought with them the Norwegian Nazi Vidkun Quisling, and could use the long Norwegian coast for their planes, their fleet, and their technical equipment.

On May 15, the Germans conquered the Netherlands, of which the royal family escaped to Canada; and on May 28, Belgium and Luxemburg.

In Hambye the house was full of family and a few friends. Our mother had requested everyone to pay his fare and to help with work.

There were still funerals attended by many people. It was considered a duty to be present when a parent, a friend, a neighbor, a person who had helped you died. But once the coffin was in the ground and the salutations exchanged, nobody was spending time with the family of the deceased.

A number of women were still requesting their husbands to bring them to church ceremonies; but as soon as these ceremonies were finished, the men hurried their wives and then their horses home quickly.

Except on these occasions, there were no vehicles on the road. Aside from the usual noises of the country, silence enveloped everything. People watched the sky in case of German airplanes.

The interest for the news on the radio had increased much. There were the ones who were listening, and there were the ones who preferred that a listener tells them in their own words and in their own voice what the news was. And the news seemed always the same: one or two ships had been sunk; they never indicated if sailors had been rescued; there was nothing to report. At least until May 10, 1940. On September 1, 1870, the German cavalry, having moved through Belgium, defeated the French emperor Napoleon III in the town of Sedan in the Ardennes Mountains. On May 10, 1940, the German tanks coming from Belgium had entered Sedan. There was no fortification there, no "Maginot Line." The German armored units had just to continue forward, down to the south, escorted by airplanes that no one was attacking.

The aim of the Germans was to capture the harbors on the English Channel. It would shorten the way to their submarines.

Now the news on the radio added to the report on sunk ships a report on the daily advance of the Germans. Here and there some units of the French army attempted to stop the Germans. But they were not equipped to resist tanks and airplanes, and too many times their officers had disappeared. It seemed that there was no French airplane.

Routine helped to live through these days. Our mother had perfectly organized her little crowd. In the morning I continued to bring water from the well and a load of logs in a wheelbarrow; then, as the other children, I got hot chocolate and well-buttered slices of bread. I rushed to fix my bed, and went from time to time with Philip to the kitchen garden to gather the green beans or the peas or any other vegetable our mother required. Afterwards, time was mine until lunch.

The two major meals were exercises in discipline. Everyone had his own seat and had to behave according to the rules of civility. The effect was calming.

In the afternoon I had to bring some more logs. If we had seen mushrooms, our mother gave us a broad basket and we went to the field where we had noted them. We were not allowed to get far from the house and we were recommended to stay near trees, so airplanes could not see us.

In the place where our paternal grandfather had planted seeds of firs many years ago, Philip and I continued to spend our hours of liberty playing with our tin soldiers, far enough from the grown-ups to feel in peace.

Our mother often joined her sisters and a young friend with red hair named Janet on the bench near the house door. At this time Taee was expressing a strong admiration for mountain troops, which had distinguished themselves in the battle of Narvik. Each of our aunts was knitting something for a nephew or for a niece, after having helped with the vegetables.

Men were not many. There was our father, the spouse of a friend of his who found difficult to mingle with the other people, and at times a third one. They were standing around, not knowing what to do. One time our mother persuaded our father to paint a landscape, an occupation that he usually liked, but the result was miserable and our mother felt that it was better to let him decide what to do. His father was not among us, as we were too many for a person of his age.

On market days our mother asked me alone to accompany her, as I was the strongest of her children and could help her at carrying what she was buying. The visits to the sister of my paternal grandmother were hasty.

On the May 10, 1940, we were pleased to hear that Neville Chamberlain, who we considered to be feeble, had resigned and was replaced as British prime minister by Winston Churchill, who had a reputation as a fighter.

The motorized army of the Germans was now moving as fast as it was possible in a country lacking serious resistance. One of its first moves was to isolate some three hundred and forty thousand allied soldiers, mostly Britons, some Belgians, and some French, in the area of the small harbor of Dunkirk, on the North Sea. Winston Churchill was not a man to let such a large number of soldiers surrender. During the whole week of May 28 to June 4, under the protection of the

Royal Air Force, they had to abandon weapons and materiel, but all embarked to England.

One sunny morning, Taee noted black smoke growing far away in the east. Theresa observed them for a while and concluded, "They have put fire on Port Jérôme refineries."

Now family and friends were watching. War had reached Le Havre and Germans would not get the oil stocked there.

"But what about us?" asked a voice.

In the afternoon we saw a band of civilians walking slowly on the road. They were mostly women and children and all looked tired. They were about forty or fifty people. They stopped at our gate. None sat. Our father enquired about them.

"We are from Calais, in the north of France. We have walked two hundred and fifty kilometers."

"Are you hungry?" asked our father. "Are there things you need?"

"We are not hungry," they replied. "We are thirsty."

"Would you like some cider," proposed our father.

"Water would be better as we still have to walk to Granville."

Granville is at a distance of twenty-four kilometers.

We the children ran to the kitchen and to the well. The poor runaways were so happy to drink some cold water. Then they left and again walked slowly.

Back in the house, our father asked our mother, "Should we do the same?"

"No," said our mother. "We are comfortable here. We have food. German airplanes attack refugees."

The next day I was more or less dreaming beneath one of these dramatic and beautiful skies of a Normandy evening when I heard fast running on the road. A single French soldier was hurrying, he too in the direction of Granville. Despite the warmth he was wearing a heavy coat, but was not carrying any weapon. Was he to embark to England in Granville? He was the only French soldier I saw this spring.

Then again it was the silence, a silence which seemed to last days after days.

On the June 10, 1940, the radio informed us that the Germans had crossed the river Seine and that the French government had abandoned Paris; also that Mussolini had declared war on France—but to us it was Mussolini, not the Italians. The following days it seemed that there was a mass exodus of all the French officials, ministers, generals, admirals, bureaucrats. Where could they go? Did they know the map of France? If they were not defending Paris, there was no city, no fortress where they could find security. This was the price to pay for lack of study and preparation, and for cowardice. They dared to announce that they would not defend Paris. The capital area and the Seine were the only places where they could hope for a successful defense. Many times in history a last defense had been waged around Paris.

I am not an early riser. For years, our father has preached the virtues of early rising. He has never persuaded me. But today there is no bread left in the house, and my mother has asked me to get to the baker's shop. The distance of three kilometers to the borough is not a long one when you cycle. To me it is still early, something like eight o'clock, and I get the light of the sun right in my eyes.

There are bright points on the road, which I believe is empty. I continue cycling and discover in front of me a long column of tanks. They don't look aggressive. They roll on the right-hand side. Each turret is open and I see the silhouette of men in light blue uniforms. Light blue was the color of the French uniforms in the past. I continue cycling and to keep my right. I am now near the first tanks. The men are not moving. The tanks continue at the same speed. But now I distinguish painted on each tank black crosses. These soldiers are German. They keep their right and do nothing to me. Therefore I continue cycling.

Now the men on tanks are wearing black uniforms. I recognize "SS," "Schutzstaffel," Hitler's soldiers. The other men were just Germans. But these "SS" behave the same as the first soldiers.

In the borough I go straight to the baker's shop. There is usually nothing interesting so early. I open the door and see four middle-aged farmers' wives and the wife of the baker all speaking quietly. They are the kind of women who have worked hard all their lives, who have given birth to several children, and who are the backbone of society in the country. The sun has colored their skin, but they don't have a single white hair. Their number in the store surprises me. Are not they afraid to get hit by a German plane? Apparently not.

Usually I wait for my turn to speak. But what I have to say seems too important to me to wait. "The Germans are here!" I utter.

The five women do not seem to have heard me. They continue speaking together.

"The Germans are here," I say again.

One of the women turns toward me and says: "You inform us that the Germans are here. Where are they?"

"There, on the main road, with their tanks," I reply.

Then the five women look at me and one goes out from the store and looks around: "Where are they?"

I repeat that they are on the main road. The women decide not to wait and go. Their husbands have probably waited enough for them in their horse-carriages. I get my bread, strap it on my bike, and go too. I see the last tanks of the column. They all seem to roll toward Granville. Then I follow the same path they have followed, but stop at our house and lay down my loaves on the kitchen table. I give the change to our mother, who thanks me. The maid shares slices. I announce again, "The Germans are here."

Nobody seems to react. It seems that they find it normal that the Germans are here. They have waited too long. Now, they believe, normal life can start again. Only my father is asking where the Germans are and I tell him that they were on the road. He says nothing.

"If the Germans are here," observed Theresa later, "we have no longer to fear their airplanes!" Everybody was pleased.

The next morning, before breakfast, Philip told me, "Let look around how things are."

At first, we only saw the garden in its summer beauty. Then, behind bushes, we distinguished a massive shape. We drew nearer. It was a tank, the gun pointing toward our house. Several young men were resting around. There was an order. They formed a short line. We heard a tabor. The men were walking at the rhythm of the instrument. A moment later they had removed their jackets and their shirts and were washing themselves at the well of one of the neighboring farmers. Three farmers' wives and their eldest daughters were considering the young men.

"They are more handsome than our men," observed one of them.

The soldiers enjoyed their curiosity. Then a wife and her daughter left, and another wife and her two daughters. Maria and two of her daughters left, but came back. Lucienne was still admiring the young men. Maria was making all kinds of cautious orders to her daughter, Lucienne was not caring. At last one of her elder sisters took her hand and obliged her to get with her inside the house.

We had seen enough and were now hurrying to get our breakfast. But a soldier stopped us and showed us the gun of the tank.

"No good, no good," he said, "boom!"

We could no longer be afraid. We were only hungry. Now every morning we heard the tabor of the Germans; also a noise we were going to hear for a few years, the noise of the nails of their black boots: a very practical noise for us, as we knew when German soldiers were around....
A sergeant formed his men in a single line, yelling more than one time to them, "*Schweinkopf*" ("pighead"). His men did not seem to mind. Henceforth, the main road in front of our house was empty during day-

time, except for a rare motorcycle, car, or truck with the letters "WH," and men in field-green watching the sky in fear of British planes. Germans were using the roads essentially at night, and their lights were reduced to a small square. There were also at night some very rare French civilian vehicles. It was wonderful to see all the stars and the moon.

On June 14, Germans were in Paris. Prime Minister Paul Reynaud attempted to organize a last resistance from Bordeaux, far in the southwest of France. But the members of parliament were just a crowd of tired, disoriented, and afraid men.

On June 18, a farmer knocked early at our door.

"In Cherbourg they have destroyed the naval dockyard and the harbor station."

Our father went to the radio and we started to listen to the British Broadcasting Corporation news from London, which reinforced what the man had said. This way we learned that hundreds of ships had steered for England, among them the SS Normandie, full of people. The next day the Germans were in Cherbourg.

Then we heard a voice full of youth, determination, and loyalty, calling for continuing the fight against the Germans along our allies. We did not know who this general was, speaking from London, by the name of Charles de Gaulle. But he seemed pretty different from the herd in Bordeaux. A supporter of the Germans, the member of Parliament Pierre Laval had succeeded in getting rid of Paul Reynaud and having full power granted to Philippe Pétain, an eighty-five-year-old marshal and admirer of Mussolini and Franco, who appointed him prime minister.

Family and friends were standing up around the set. Not many sentences were said. Attitudes were clear: there were the prudent and there were the enthusiasts, the smaller number. From this time we listened less and less to Radio Paris, but did not stop entirely as it provided practical information. More and more people in France hummed: "Radio Paris ment." ("Radio Paris lies.")

"Radio Paris est allemand." ("Radio Paris is German.")

Pétain and Laval negotiated an armistice; organized a "National Movement" to support them; and allowed the Japanese, the allies of the Germans, to use the airports in the then French colony of Indochina. Germans could use the harbors of Brest, Lorient, Saint-Nazaire, La Rochelle, and Bordeaux to send their submarines to attack British and Canadian convoys in the Atlantic Ocean. The administration in France was led by friends of the Germans. Alsace was incorporated to Germany, discreetly.

It was through the BBC that we heard about an extraordinary proposal by Winston Churchill: to have only one nationality for French and Britons.

In Normandy it was nothing new. This was how things were when the duchy, the kingdom, and other parts were bound together. For three days Normans remained silent. None among them discussed the proposal. Normans are a practical people, and after the lapse of three days continued as if the proposal had not been made. In Brittany, some people organized to get their independence. . . .

Soon it appeared that the Germans wished to have a peaceful population. Their soldiers had been ordered to be "correct" toward the civilians. Much of what they wanted was done by the French administration and the French police, discreetly. Many French soldiers still in their units were not taken as prisoners, but were demobilized.

7

Adapting

I stop my bike and sit at the skirt of a little wood. Our mother gave me a banknote of twenty marks. I look at the greenish little piece of paper and wonder if I can buy anything with it.

Again I ride my bicycle. There is a poster on the wall of the post office. I come near it. It is divided by a vertical line. On the left it is in German, "Bekanmarung," on the right in French, "Avis." I learn that ten men have been shot as reprisals, because one German had been killed. I read the names of the victims. So it is true: every time a German is killed, they shoot ten Frenchmen.

I go in and ask for some stamps. The employee gives me stamps of which the value has been reduced by half. The French Republic has been replaced by the French State. The employee does not seem surprised by my German banknote and gives me my change for it—in French coins.

I am at the same place, but it is a different country. In addition to our sign-posts, there are now wood posts indicating directions in black on white.

As our mother said, there is food in Hambye. Bread is not plentiful, but there are potatoes. Coffee is replaced by roasted barley. There is less sugar. Cocoa has disappeared. But in Hambye there are plenty of foods city people are deprived of. So our mother has now started to send parcels to family and friends, mostly butter, which is in high demand and can be used to get something else. Every market day she goes to the post office and sends her parcels registered; some of them go to city postmen, who are distributing her other parcels.

Eggs are plentiful and it is still easy at this time to buy meat.

Some other goods are difficult to get. Only certain car drivers, such as physicians, can obtain some gas. There is no soap and it is becoming a major inconvenience.

Germans who did not have much gas were prompt to reestablish trains and railways, so they could use them too.

Little by little family and friends left the house of my paternal grandfather.

France still had a powerful fleet. The question was if it would support the Germans or the Allies. Winston Churchill gave the order to sink it, if it would not join the British fleet. Alas, French navy officers had been educated to despise Britons.

On July 3, 1940, a British squadron requested the two French battleships and the two French battle cruisers in the harbor of Mers-el-Kébir, Algeria, to join it, otherwise they would be sunk. Admiral Marcel-Bruno Gensoul refused to join the British squadron and twelve hundred French sailors got killed.

On the same day, twenty-three days after Dunkirk, Britons seized French war ships in Portsmouth and Plymouth and in Alexandria, Egypt; they fought on the battleship Richelieu in Dakar, Senegal.

When we heard this news, we said nothing. It was too heavy.

Men were still not many. There was no question of sending me back to Agneaux. After some discussion, our parents decided that our young brothers and sisters would attend school in Hambye, and that Philip and I would accompany our father in Montreuil-sous-bois and attend a school in Paris, where they probably had more qualified teachers. In Normandy, a great number of male professional teachers were kept prisoners by the Germans.

From time to time a German truck passed on the road; less often, the car of one of the two physicians in Hambye. We heard only the sounds of the country in summer. It seemed that there was a new kind of normalcy. Farmers were taking their wives and some other people to the Tuesday markets, and to church on Sunday mornings in their horse carriages. Less was offered to customers in the market, and even less in the grocery stores. The Roman Catholic Church recruited its clergy from among locals, and these days it was definitely an asset as Norman priests knew how to speak to Norman worshippers. They had gained in authority.

There was as much meat as before in the stores of the two butchers. It was clear that the controls did not work for them, and no inspector dared to draw near them. It was the same all through the country. So our mother went to Leconte and, to the butcher's surprise, asked for all the beef fat he possessed. And the man became happy when our mother said to him that instead of paying him, she would give him some soap. On the following Sunday our father carried away this fat to his manufacture and mixed it with soda in cake-tins. His soap was in high demand very quickly.

We the children were more concerned through enjoying our new liberty. There was no plane to fear and we could run everywhere. We brought to our mother large baskets of mushrooms and of blackberries. We helped the farmers a little. And I cleaved wood as there was no man to do it.

We heard that Hitler had decided to prepare a landing operation against England. The distance from Calais to Dover is only about twenty miles. But as he had not prevented the British, the French, and the Belgian soldiers stranded on the beach of Dunkirk from escaping to England, and had not used this opportunity to land in Britain, we did not believe that Germans would be able to cross the Channel on ships.

This was not the opinion of Marshal Hermann Göring, chief of the German Air Force. From August 8, he sent hundreds of planes over England. On August 15, he had a thousand planes aggressing in a bright summer sky during the whole day. This week and the following ones, London, Coventry, Birmingham, and other cities were bombed day and night. On August 18, there was an intense battle. The fighters of Stanley Baldwin, moving in groups of three, opposed the German bombers and fighters.

On such days, we could observe the fringe of the battle at twelve thousand to fifteen thousand feet in altitude. To us it was safe. But up there we could see from time to time a black smoke rising from a plane, which fell down quickly; we could see parachutes moving down like cut white flowers. Following long moments, we the children were looking at the sky without sharing the drama.

We were getting ready to go to bed when we heard big bangs on the door. In a dark night without wind, two farmers asked for a bike. They explained that it was to help a British pilot. I went outside and brought my bicycle from the garage. Our father and I followed the farmers and we discovered the airman standing up in the middle of hay in a barn in the company of the son of one of the farmers. He could not speak French. We could not speak English. But he was pleased when he saw the bike. One of the farmers went on the other bike I had seen on the hay and made a gesture of invitation to do the same to the pilot. The two men disappeared quickly in the darkness. Three days later I got my bike back. The pilot had been helped by a fisherman in Granville; driving a wood boat, they had been lucky to find, not too far, a British submarine.

Every time the weather was fit, Germans continued to bomb cities and airports in Britain. But the blitz could not last past September 15, as this time the area of the Channel is windy and rainy. Germans returned to their owners the river barges in which they had hoped to transport troops to Britain. . . .

They had, then, to help their Italian allies, who were trying to invade Greece. But at the time, Philip and I were starting a new life in Montreuil-sous-bois and Paris.

Tired from our trip, we ate in the evening some of the food we had brought from Hambye in our cardboard suitcases. The next day our father registered us in Voltaire high school and in a scout association, which would keep us busy six days of the week. Then he rushed to city hall in Montreuil-sousbois to get food coupons for us. Some of these coupons were useless, as nobody was selling a number of the corresponding foods. With the exception of the baker's and the haberdashery, where I could buy a few books and some tin soldiers, the market and the stores were offering little. At least that was what it looked like.

Our father had bought all the cigarettes he could for his coupons. Then he set apart some packs for his own consumption, and went with us to the grocery store on the opposite side of the street. There was a bar with a few bottles, but nothing on the tables or in the boxes on the ground. Our father presented some coupons and got some wine in exchange. Then he showed his packs of cigarettes to the merchant. The man counted them and then went to a room behind the store and came back with potatoes. My father paid and indicated that he could in the future barter some soap. We saw in the eyes of the merchant that our father had become a serious customer for him. Back home our father added the bottles of red wine he had bought to several other bottles of red wine. I asked him why he had so many bottles of wine. "To barter" was his answer.

The helper in Montreuil-sous-bois, Mrs. Lahr, was happy to see us again, especially Philip, who at the time was barely ten years old. Alone with two black dogs, she had again this young boy to take care of.

The school and the scouts were just a few minutes from home with the subway. Voltaire had been a philosopher who had forbidden the king and the church to do injustice against people. At the time of German occupation, to use his name for our school was a great symbol. There was a portrait of Marshal Pétain in each classroom. The music teacher tried to make me and the other twenty students in our classroom sing what he had been told to make us sing:

"Maréchal, nous voilà,

Nous, l'espoir de la France . . . "

("Marshall, there we are,

We, the hope of France . . .")

And we sang:

"Maréchal, nous voià,

Nous, les poires (the pears) de la France . . . "

("Marshall, there we are,

We, the pears of France . . .")

We had other variations for "l'espoir."

No student said "le Maréchal Pétain." Usually they called him "le vieux" (the old one).

I had chosen English for the study of a modern language. We learned nothing from the teacher we had been assigned. But all the other men in charge of us were competent and able teachers. It was the same for Philip and his fellow students. Our parents had been right.

Our father had also been wise in not telling us that the scout movement was forbidden. Philip was with a group of juniors. My own group was of about two dozen boys from twelve to fifteen years old. For the first part of the year we met in a large room; later, in the woods. Our leaders were two young men, a little afraid of getting caught when they were with us in the city. We learned much from them too, and it made for excellent camping. We liked their choice of songs, and we were pleased to sing them while walking in uniforms where there were no Germans.

At home I had been put in charge of buying some bread every day at noon, when Philip and I ate at home before returning to school. I felt so hungry that I always ate some of the bread I had bought. As for other food, it was rutabaga for two weeks, then Jerusalem artichokes for one week alternatively. Our father tried to get some other vegetables, but with little success. The parcels from our mother were really welcome.

On certain weekends our father was in Laval, visiting his own father, who had even less than us to eat. Seniors had been declared "useless mouths" by the men in Vichy. We remembered the thousands and thousands of young men Pétain had sent to their deaths under German shells and without any hope of success during the First World War. The brother of our grandfather, Emile, had been a victim of these massacres.

Our mother was already sending butter to our paternal grandfather and his helper, but she knew that she had to do more. Was not she now living in his family house in Hambye? When he was in Laval, our father visited farms around to get eggs, poultry, and whatever he could for his father. When winter came, our grandfather was still not eating enough and he had very little wood. Our father felt a feeling of urgency and visited every place he thought he could barter some soap or even some butter to get fuel for his father. Happily, he became successful.

At school in Paris, the "Secours National" ("The National Rescue") distributed every morning to each student two crackers and a vitamin pill. It helped just a little, especially the students who did not have the time for a breakfast. Some of our fellow students were really suffering from hunger. Our father, Philip, and I were fortunate to get this butter to spread on our bread. At Christmas it was good to be back in Hambye.

The large room with eight beds and the kitchen with its big black stove were warm; the food was abundant and varied; we were the seven children with our parents. For this Christmas there were few presents, only for the youngest ones. But we knew it could not be different.

There was barely any snow in the country. Planes were now absent from the sky. The dampness was making the cold bitter. The great winds of the fall had stopped. Days were short. Smoke from the farms' stacks showed there was still life in the silent country. Our father had returned to Montreuil-sous-bois for his work. Philip visited his friends, and he had many since he had attended school in Hambye. His preference was to stay in Hambye and not go back to Voltaire high school. No adult was concerned by his opinions or his choices. I tried to help my mother start the fire in the kitchen stove each morning, bringing water from the pump, wood from the shed, greens from the kitchen garden, eggs from the farms, bread from the borough, and mailing her parcels of butter at the post office. But I spent as much time as possible by the stove reading books from our paternal grandfather's library. It seemed to me that our two sisters were looking at Philip and me as some kind of intruders.

At the end of the holidays, our father escorted Philip and me back to Montreuil-sous-bois. He had carried many butter parcels to distribute to our helper Mrs. Lahr, to a few friends and to coworkers, and some more to barter. Mrs. Lahr's eyes sparkled when he added a little piece of soap to the butter he had given to her. Our father had also brought what our mother was calling "milk jam." Philip and I helped him, but we had found it laborious to walk from the train inside the subway and then to our house.

We were no longer waiting for milk in Montreuil-sous-bois. Standing in line was cold. It was rare that there was some milk for us. When we boiled it, it turned into water with white filaments. One morning, people in the line shoved discreetly to look at the shoes of a man among us.

And these shoes were good walking shoes. We all stop speaking. Our mother had put her milk jam into clean, fourteen-ounce tin paint cans provided by our father from his manufacturer. The liquid inside was of a light brown color, and delicious. We used it in our barley decoction of the morning, feeling grateful to our mother. Of course soon we had exhausted our supply. But our breakfasts were our real meals of the day.

It was hard for Philip and me to do schoolwork every evening but Thursdays and Sundays. We did not get much heat from a small electric heater. It happened that an old man of the passive defense whistled at us because some light was visible from our windows. Sometimes this man entered into the house. It was forbidden to lock doors. Philip and I were getting bored from hearing his lectures. We did not realize that lights on the ground could be dangerous to us. We knew that there were no Germans in the eastern part of the Parisian area except in Vincennes, kilometers from us. At times there was an alert. We could see the searchlights moving through the night sky and hear the double detonations of the antiaircraft guns. Soon it turned into an opportunity to observe the stars, which are so beautiful.

Our teachers did not speak about the war. Even the music teacher became more interested in tunes with no relation with the events. As a matter of fact, it seemed that at this time, in the first months of 1941, nothing was happening but in Greece, and that the British were keeping the Germans away from Egypt and the Suez Canal. Allied airplanes were nearly daily above Le Havre, bombing here, bombing there, but our grandmother did not believe the situation to be of grave concern. In consequence I went to spend my Easter holidays in her house.

Gabrielle was waiting for me at the arrival of the train in Le Havre and led me to a car. It was empty. Gabrielle told me that Alexander (our grandmother's driver and also a Russian grand duke) along with his wife and their eight children had preferred not to wait for the Germans, and that some French military had seized the two cars of my grandmother. The car Gabrielle was driving belonged to the Ateliers Doré.

The large house on Francis the First Boulevard seemed empty, even though a maid was cleaning the steps of the hall. My grandmother was trying to hide it, but she had started a period of worrying. Getting food or fuel was not difficult for her. In Les Hellandes her gardener made sure she got enough of the first for her and her family; by their nature the Ateliers Doré could provide her with plenty of wood and some of the gas the municipality was allocating them. Germans, despite their suspicions, were allowing fishermen to go out to sea during the night.

Nobody explained to me what was the situation of the Ateliers Doré. Most of their employees were war prisoners. A few had gone to England and a few were hiding; the older ones had stayed, but there was no ship in the harbor to give them work. Le Havre normally lived from the seas during peace.

Theresa was pleased to inform me about the war in Greece and in North Africa. Her mother had allowed her to keep a dog, a white terrier, for her protection. My grandmother did not like animals in her house.

8
They Take Shelter in Our Houses

A German admiral had requisitioned a bedroom on the second floor of my grandmother's house. Theresa refused to leave her own bedroom on the same floor, as this admiral was drinking two bottles of Benedictine every day. Having sailors but no ship in Le Havre, wearing a royal blue coat with plenty of golden cordons and a two-foot long sword, he kept repeating:

"Deutschland, kaput!" ("Germany, broken down!")

My grandmother was afraid he would fall in the stairs, so drunk he was.

Allied airplanes were flying daily over Le Havre. At times they were bombing here and there. German planes were gone.

German soldiers and sailors were rare in the center. They were hiding underground. The Todt Organization slaves had built for them powerful bunkers they had camouflaged like houses along the seashore. The Germans had equipped them with machine guns and big guns. They had dug galleries between these bunkers and the ones that they had in the cliff, housed several thousand soldiers and sailors. One morning Gabrielle, Theresa, and I were surprised to see eight German soldiers doing the goose step on the boulevard. We were observing them from a window of the red bedroom when we saw them run to a large door on the other side of the street; nearly immediately two Polish fighters were at the level of our floor. The pilots had had the time to see us and made a gesture of salute to us. It was good to feel them so near. Polish aviators had already gained a reputation of bravery and daring.

During these holidays I used to spend my mornings with Gabrielle, who fixed my breakfast with true milk from my grandmother's cows in Les Hellandes and who took me to different places among the streets of the city. After lunch, prepared under the direction of my grandmother and eaten with her and her daughters on a usual white tablecloth, Theresa took care of me. She continued to explain to me the war events, now in North Africa, where the British were starting to get rid of Marshal Erwin Rommel and his tanks and to control the sky too. More and more Canadian bombers were now flying directly from North America to Britain. A couple of times Theresa came with me to one of the bathrooms, where she washed her dog. The animal seemed to enjoy the treatment. At the end Theresa had to wrap it up quickly in a towel before it would shake water all over the place.

During the two weeks of the holidays Theresa led me to the seashore every afternoon. There she put a few towels on the shingles, the same as the other women who were exposing their bodies to the sun had done. Theresa had a pack of cards and, with the dog near us, we played party after party of twenty-one. Then we made the dog run until we were home.

Back in Montreuil-sous-bois, the cold had gone. Hunger was around. Some students were very thin. At noon, getting back home from Voltaire high school, Philip and I pressed our fists against our stomachs. Mrs. Lahr had prepared the same rutabagas cooked in water and we had to make an effort to eat them. Mrs. Lahr had had no choice, as rutabagas were, most days, the only vegetables sold. Happily we had some bread portions.

May is such a beautiful month in the Parisian area. We had gotten gas masks. But youths younger than the preceding years were going to the woods on their bikes and coming back with sweet-smelling bunches of lily of the valley. White-haired people had become rare. There were many other people spending time around outside tables at restaurants. But May seems to be also the time for war. On the 8th, the destroyer Bulldog had captured a submarine; on the 27th, the battleship Bismarck had been sunk. Bombings continued through Europe.

An enormous surprise was to hear that on June 22, Germans and their small European allies had sent three million soldiers on a front of two thousand miles against Soviet Union. They claimed that on the first day they had destroyed eight hundred Soviet airplanes on the ground and four hundred in the air. It seemed unreal. It was so big, so massive. And Germans were in trouble in Africa and had failed to invade Britain. Later we learned that the leader of the German navy, Admiral Erich Raeder, had opposed extending the war into Russia.

Soon it appeared that the Soviet forces were not up to par. They were lacking officers, as many had been recently eliminated. They were using horse-drawn guns instead of bombers, individual guns instead of machine guns, and had too few tanks, themselves of poor quality and easily destroyed. Germans seemed to have no difficulty advancing, considering the speed of their tanks.

A few people asked me if I had read *War and Peace* by Tolstoy. No, I had not. They did not comment.

Little by little the lack of good roads was slowing the speed of tanks, trucks and motorcycles. German vehicles could not penetrate in the vast Pripet Marsh. Germans had not enough soldiers to man the whole front. Guerillas were circulating unseen between the nests of their machine guns. German lines of communication were becoming fragile. The Soviet Union had started to produce a superior tank, the fast and invulnerable T-34s.

In Western Europe, older Germans were replacing the young soldiers sent to the east. Czechs, Romanians, and other non-Germans were replacing Germans. Germans were depleting their armies in Western Europe. There was a dispute in their navy that twelve hundred sailors were more effective aboard forty or fifty submarines than aboard one battleship. The Todt Organization was bringing more and more slaves from all over Europe to build a stronger "Atlantic Wall" and stronger submarine shelters.

In the east, Germans continued to use terror. In the west, they shot a few young men for having tried to get to Britain or for sabotage. In France, they used the government of Pétain; a few officers in each "département" were enough to have the prefects and their personnel doing whatever they wanted. On the other hand, now the Communists were in the resistance; but the people in general noted that Germans were becoming absent.

Our parents decided that I would spend the first month of the summer holidays in the Alps to have the good air of the mountains prevent me from getting tuberculosis, a frequent ailment at the time. I boarded a train to Saint Gervais le Fayet, in Savoy, near the Italian border. I had not seen mountains and was impressed by their size and their immobility. The sea is always alive. These masses of stone never change.

Two slim persons, a married couple, were waiting for me and some children I did not know. They greeted us and told us to take our luggage. We started to walk slowly. It was flat for a while; then we took a small climbing road and arrived at a two-floor house with a small garden and some trees around. On arrival we were requested to provide our food coupons for one month and then shown our bedrooms.

My room on the second floor was quite small but had a view towards the "Mont Blanc." I washed myself and went down to the dining room for my first meal. Around our two hosts were a dozen silent children. Everybody seemed shy. The meal was not abundant, but made of different vegetables. I was a bit hungry when I left. Our hosts had no program for us and told us to do whatever we liked, provided that we stayed near the house. I started to explore. There was nothing to retain my attention. In the house, there was no book and no game. The following day was a long one for me as our hosts continued to show no initiative. But the day after, they decided to show us the village.

It was a perfect sunny day. We arrived at a little stone bridge. Six young men, looking like farm boys, clad in the same poor green canvas and with hats with cock feathers, were standing against the parapet, plainly not knowing what to do. I was told that they were Italians, but that people did not worry as they were quiet. Merchants added with pity that they had no money. I had never seen a torrent before and was impressed by the speed of the water and the strong declivity. Arriving downtown, I would have liked to buy something to read, but had little money myself and decided to save it. Everybody seemed to tell us to watch the "Mont Blanc."

After a few other empty days the man who was our host decided to take us "in the mountain." At his slow pace, we climbed and climbed. The landscape was becoming more and more open. Stone was alternating with pasture. There was no fence. The rocks had beautiful dark blue and grey colors. The children had good legs and seemed pleased. At last our host stopped and invited us to contemplate the view of the valley, the mountains, and the sky. And we started to descend. Climbing up had not required much effort, but descending seemed to hurt more and more our knees, as the whole body hammered with each step. Our host never took us again for another walk. I had to make myself busy. My explorations led me to a wood full of raspberry bushes. Their fruits were ripe and for a few days I gorged like a young bear. But I did not like to stay in a place where I did not know what was going on. I had had enough with my time in boarding schools. Back in Montreuil-sous-bois, I rushed to a bookstore. *War and Peace* was not available, but I discover a translation of Hitler's book, *Mein Kampf*, and bought a copy of it.

In Hambye I discovered that our mother had started to raise rabbits and was often called by the two local physicians because of her training as a nurse. The butcher was still on friendly terms with our parents and provided our mother with the fat used by our father for his soap. He was pleased to get some soap for his fat. And he was selling meat relatively freely, but only to people he was sure who would not denounce him. To strangers, he sold meat only for the quantity their coupons entitled them. When the farmers around our family house killed a pig or another animal, they always shared with their neighbors. In this way no one denounced them, and the farmers who had received meat from them gave them meat in return; our parents could not give meat, but soap and paint. Farmers continued not to declare all their newborn animals, and they raised them secretly. On certain fences they advertised "hoof-and-mouth disease," which had the effect of making both Germans and officials afraid.

Our mother used her rabbits for both their meat and their skin. As she could not send as much meat as she wished to people she was helping, she now sent them rabbit meat. Of course this meat was also for her immediate family. She exchanged the skins of animals recently killed with skins which had been prepared, and made warm clothes for her children and herself with those skins. For me, the result was that as soon as I arrived in Hambye I was committed to cleaning the cages once a week and helping my brother Philip and our sisters to find food for them. This pleased another woman, Louise, who helped our mother with additional tasks, but found heavy the manure from the rabbits.

Germans were too afraid of allied airplanes to use the roads by day. If they did, one of their soldiers would lie on the side of their vehicle, constantly watching the sky. So the roads were now, during the day, fully ours. Soon we were walking a lot on them; the maid was not afraid to occupy their middle with the five youngest children of our mother. Philip and I discovered that we could visit many places with our bikes.

I had started to read *Mein Kampf*, and to discover in its pages an inhabitant of the former Austrian Empire, German-speaking like his emperor, but among a majority of Slavic and Hungarian peoples and often with a Jewish leadership. At the peace of Versailles, Austria had been separated from its non-German-speaking parts. But this did not satisfy Hitler. For him, Austria should have kept all its former territory and the non-German-speaking people should have disappeared. So his dream was of a huge "Lebens Raum" ("vital space") for Germans. He justified his claim by writing that Germans belonged to a superior race and that certain races such as the Slavs and the Jews were only "Untermenschen" (people of inferior races). Just recently, in other countries, slavery was tolerated because certain races were considered "inferior." I was only thirteen years old, but it seemed to me that these theories were wrong morally and scientifically, and extremely dangerous.

Germans had not disappeared. Now they were living in our houses. In the borough of Hambye we had a great uncle who possessed a large house. He was a bachelor. At the time Germans requisitioned houses, he was not in Hambye. So the Germans took his whole house and threw in the fire most of his furniture. When he came back he complained and was authorized to use a small part of his house with his furniture that had not been burned.

Germans requisitioned a small room and our parents' room in our family house in the country. They transformed the small room into an office with telephones; they used the bedroom only in warm weather as it was not heated. They installed a telephone line from our attic. The tank with its gun towards the house—was it the same one or another one?—was still on the same spot. Soldiers came in and out of our kitchen, as it was in the traditional manner the entrance room. Quite often they used the heat of the stove for their own cooking. Our mother did not protest, but diplomatically helped them to prepare better food. So they treated her with a certain respect. And it gave us the opportunity to inform them about news their own media were trying to hide. But it was making it difficult for our mother to cook our meals.

There were no Germans in Montreuil-sous-bois and generally east of the Parisian area, where they were afraid of the Communists. Often we had a walk to the castle of Vincennes, a fourteenth-century royal fortress surrounded by many trees. Like the French had done, the Germans continued to use it as barracks and depot. In the cafés and restaurants, they have never been as many as their predecessors. At times we saw none of them.

9

We Too Are Men

I had excellent teachers this year. One of them was Mr. Massinon, a blind man about seventy-five years old, escorted by a young assistant, in charge of teaching us French, Latin, and Greek. He was in love with the old Mediterranean world that he knew intimately. To us he recited poems, mostly in Greek, and showed us their connection with the landscape, the people, the history, and the traditions. Often he moved from such a poem to one in French, showing us the similitude of the inspiration or of the roots of a drama. He was with us on all the little roads of Sicily, south Italy, great Greece, walking, accompanying the donkey-drawn carts, with paints representing Orlando Furioso, of the locals. He was with us on the small boats of the fishermen drawing near all the islands poets and writers had spoken about. He was with Ulysses when he met Nausikaa, with Xenophon when his soldiers, tired out by their long march through the land of Asia, at last saw the sparkling of the sun on water and shouted: "Thalassa! Thalassa!" ("The sea! The sea!")

Mr. Massinon pointed out to us that Greeks were and are still sailors. His choices of French texts mixed adventure, admiration for girls, and feelings for the beauty of nature. Nothing could speak better to the hearts of thirteen- and fourteen-year-old boys. When the time came to end the lecture, we asked him to continue and he did, because he loved what he was teaching.

In the same year, I had for the first time a teacher who made me understand mathematics. We had no music teacher, but a drawing teacher who showed us how to use charcoal and to understand the adjustment and the proportions of the human body, and the anarchical tendencies of the artists.

We were already seated in our classroom when a man with very few hairs and wearing a cape entered. Was he sixty years old? Soon we understood why he was wearing a cape. He gave a push to it and a pile of worn-out red books appeared. He laid them aside on the desk and asked us:

"Do you know the Lake District, in Northern England?"

We looked at him with astonishment. We had heard so much about the Greeks and the Romans, but England was unknown to us.

"It is a beautiful area, where nature is at its best. The eighteenth century in England was a time for industrialization and some men tried to escape from its pollution. They settled in the Lake District."

We had never heard about industrialization and pollution. But our teacher tried to explain to us that for the English Romantics nature was a protection, an informing and spiritual influence on life. None of our studies had prepared us to understand this language. Observing our incertitude, the teacher rose on his feet and told us: "To introduce you to the thinking of the English Romantics, I am going to recite to you a poem by William Wordsworth, 'The Daffodils':

'I wandered lonely as a cloud
That floats on high o'er vales and hills,

When all at once I saw a crowd,
A host, of golden daffodils;
Beside the lake, beneath the trees,
Fluttering and dancing in the breeze.'"

He continued to recite and arrived at the last strophe:

"For oft, when on my couch I lie
In vacant or in pensive mood,
They flash upon that inward eye
Which is the bliss of solitude;
And then my heart with pleasure fills,
And dances with the daffodils."

We had not understood at all the sense of the poem. Our English was too poor. But we had admired the beauty of the sounds. We understood that we were facing a great language, and that gave us the will to learn it. It was exactly what the Vichy propaganda was dissuading us to do.

The teacher then started to distribute his red books, telling us that we would learn something by using them. Then he commentated on the poem that we had heard and we felt that we were starting to learn a new language, a new country, and some philosophy. This teacher came back a couple of times. Then we learned that he had been dismissed. A saboteur replaced him, making sure we would learn nothing of the English language and civilization.

On October 28, 1941, came the interdiction to listen to the British Broadcasting Corporation from London. This was expected and we would continue whatever. We trusted the BBC because it reported losses as well as gains, and did not inflate figures. It did not hesitate, for instance, to say later in November that German submarines had sunk the aircraft carrier Ark Royal and the battleship Barham, and again in

December the cruiser Galatea, and then two other ones. It was the BBC that informed us that German submarines had sunk in October a U.S. destroyer. It was an act of war against a neutral country, which could be followed by severe sanctions. In December, it announced a cut of fifty percent in German navy fuel quotas; individually Germans confirmed that it was already in force, and that similar reductions were expected for tanks and airplanes. The BBC also told us that Germans had arrived within twenty-five miles of Moscow.

In the morning of December 7, 1941, Japanese airplanes made a surprise attack against the U.S. Pacific fleet, which was anchored in Pearl Harbor, in Hawaii, and against Midway, Wake, and Guam. The next day the Japanese attacked Hong Kong, defended by Canadians and Indians. We heard also about other Japanese attacks, such as on the Philippines and Darwin, in Australia. The same day, their airplanes sunk the *Prince of Wales* and the *Repulse*. Now we knew that the United States was in the war, now extended to the world, and that both Germany and Japan would be defeated.

German soldiers had started to tell us terrible stories. They were not equipped for the Russian winter. They had no parkas and other warm clothes; their boots did not protect their feet like the Russian ones; their machine guns did not work in the cold; their tanks and their airplanes were becoming more and more difficult to operate against the Soviet ones. They were throwing away their submachine guns when they could find a Kalashnikov. Guerillas were attacking their supplies.

It was clear that Hitler and his gang had not read *War and Peace*, and did not know what General Mikhail Kutuzov knew, that the greatest general of Russia had for a name *winter*. In November 1941, Russians took back Rostov; on December 6, their T-34s were starting to encircle the Germans before Moscow.

It was good to spend the two weeks of the Christmas holidays in the family house in Hambye, in the warmth of the wood fires and with much good food, in the midst of our family. However, our mother had discovered lice in our hair. There was a lotion to apply against them, called "Marie-Rose." But soon the supply in pharmacies was exhausted and we had to use vinegar instead. As the latter did not help against it, we used small toothcombs. Still we had to scratch ourselves. We would endure them until the Germans would be gone.

Back in Montreuil-sous-bois, Philip and I noticed that there too everybody was carrying lice. It did not take many days for our hands and our ears to turn blue because of cold and hunger. We had an allowance of fifty kilos of coal per month. It was too little for heating the house more than a couple of days. Our father, at certain times, burned books with large editions in one of the fireplaces. But we only got an illusion of heat. The best was to stay in bed, but our clocks reminded us that it was time to get up to prepare ourselves for school or something else.

One of our fellow students, Martin, thought that we did not have enough fun at school. So he and three other students hid along the path of the two students who were bringing a box of crackers to the 4-C class and captured their box. That morning we were very pleased to get twice as many crackers than as usual. But in the afternoon we had a visit of the principal, who told us that we had acted egoistically and that it was our duty to share. The next day there were no crackers for us.

A week later, as we had spent instruction time in the shelter of the school on the eve, we were asked to board the trucks at the door. Each of us was wearing an armband with the stamp of the school.

The trucks took us to Boulogne-Billancourt, where there was a car factory and a city. Now there was no street. Tractors had made a track among the debris. Our task was to try to find children who could still be under the rubble. Each of us had to explore a small square of ground. We had been given shovels, but they were of no use. We were moving the rubbish with care with our hands.

A tall, slim woman in a dark blue uniform and a large beret seemed to be in charge of the operations. In moving on a central form, she presented on all sides an impeccable outline. I stopped my work to contemplate her. Suddenly I realized that she was wearing a uniform of the "Mouvement National." I felt ashamed of myself, and simultaneously all my body was full of desire for her. Getting back to my task, I gathered a tin soldier who, in my opinion, would fit perfectly in my collection. But for the second time I became ashamed: I was not going to take anything that belonged to a victim of the bombing.

Then I noted a very big, dark blue object in a corner. Not knowing what to do, I referred to our leader. He came back quickly a moment later.

"There are bombs which have not yet exploded. Get back to the trucks!"

One hour later we were in our classrooms. For the first time we had seen the result of a heavy bombing.

The next time an alert was made, Martin said loudly, "I am not going back to the basement of the school, for waiting and having nothing to do. I am going to the Père Lachaise Cemetery. There is no reason to bomb a cemetery. They are already dead."

The Père Lachaise cemetery is large. We thought that no airplane would see us under its many trees. A moment later we were all the class among the tombs, walking slowly, reading what was inscribed on the stones. Little by little we forgot where we were and spoke about many different topics. At the end of the alert we went back to the school. Nobody had noted our absence. From that day on, we spent the time of each alert in the cemetery.

We were all in need of new clothes and new shoes. But we had to continue to wear what we owned, as it was difficult to get clothes and shoes. Coupons were for very little. Lucky were the people who had unused old clothes, as they could be transformed by a tailor or a seamstress.

Shoes were nearly impossible to get. A lot of time was devoted to repair, especially socks. Happily, yarn and needles remained available.

January of 1942 was a cold month. We really needed clothes. In Hambye our mother made jackets of rabbit fur for my younger brothers and sisters. In Montreuil-sous-bois, what we could do was introduce newspapers between our shirts and our jackets, but they had a tendency to fall down all the time. Germans were looking for copper to make their munitions. They started to unbolt bronze statues. All through Europe, people had to pay a tax of a certain weight of copper. In Montreuil-sous-bois, our father removed several lamps and brought their metal to city hall. But in Hambye, Laval, and Le Havre, my mother and my grandparents did nothing. Curious, I inquired carefully around and little by little discovered that most people had done nothing too.

Time to time, in the cities, small sheets of poor paper arrived in the mailboxes, letting us know that the Resistance was growing.

Germans had kept French war prisoners in Saint-Lô, near Hambye, and in Cherbourg. Norman families appreciated being able to meet fiancés, husbands, sons, and brothers. But we heard from people visiting Paris that on January 20 and 24, these prisoners had been put aboard forty-eight cattle cars and sent to Germany. Women demonstrated in vain with songs.

On February 9, 1942, I was waiting for my turn at the barber in Montreuil-sous-bois. Four men, fifty or sixty years old, had arrived before me. I liked to see the barber's wife, Madame Jean as we called her. She was a medium-size, well-built, lively woman, with dancing earrings under her long black hair, officially in charge of making customers pay. When I had arrived, she had vanished through the door at the bottom of the store. Then minutes later she reappeared and uttered with her Aquitanian accent we were fond of, "The MS Normandie has been burnt down in New York harbor and has capsized. . . . "

We looked at each other one in the store. At last one of the men said with contained angriness, "It is the pro-German people. . . . "

"There are many there," said one of the other men.

"They should put all them in jail," commentated another customer.

It was dangerous to speak too much and we all stopped. I was getting full of sadness. "How could they have done such a crime?"

"In a way," commentated the first man, "no one has been killed." He gave a look to Madame Jean. "Think, if she would have been sank in the middle of the Atlantic, with thousands of people on board. . . . "

"It would not have happened in Soviet Union," said the second man.

"How do you know?" said the third man.

This was the end of the conversation. At last the barber Monsieur Jean took care of me. He was a tall, lean man, with dark eyes deep-set under black brows and entirely bald, quite older than Madame Jean and looking very in love with her. There was not any shampoo, and the barber could not clean his instruments as there was no product to do it. In this manner, we could receive the lice of the previous customers. However, Monsieur Jean used to massage flexibly our heads and this provided us with relaxation.

A few days later, on February 16, the Pétain government in Vichy issued a statute instituting the compulsory work service for all young men aged sixteen years old and above. At school, the immediate reaction was to discuss about the ways to escape from it. We were pleased that the United States had entered the war, but we wondered about their capacity as so many ships were sank along their coasts. The destruction of the new powerful German radar north of Le Havre by Scottish paratroopers in the night of February 27-28, 1942, and British-Canadian raid on the March 27 and 28, in the same year, however, gave us hope. A destroyer had been blown up against the gates of the large dock of Saint-Nazaire, the only one the battleship Tirpitz could use outside Germany. The British and the Canadians had not abandoned Europe.

THE FIVE SISTERS

When I arrived at Le Havre for my Easter holidays, I got surprised by how dark my grandmother's house was. The bombings had broken most of the panes of glass of the windows. As it was vain to replace them, my grandmother had them replaced with plywood.

Back to Montreuil-sous-bois, we got the visit of our mother. She had assembled coupons to get clothes for Philip and for me. She also bought us wood soles with cardboard thongs; it was not easy to walk in them, but there was room for our feet.

10
To Hold

It was difficult to be a scout with wood soles fixed with cardboard lashes. I had worked in the kitchen garden of our mother in wood clogs, but they were not fit for even going to school, and they hurt my feet. One evening in Montreuil-sous-bois a man came who drew the shape of each of my feet on white sheets of paper. A few days later, our father joined us for lunch time, which was not in his habit, when the man who had measured my feet rang our bell. He came with a splendid pair of walking shoes. I tried them. They fit perfectly and the leather was supple and pleasant. Our father paid the man, dearly. I was surprised. Never had I so beautiful and agreeable shoes.

Philip got my old leather shoes, repaired by a shoemaker. Our older sister got Philip's shoes, properly adjusted, and so on for every child of our parents. By definition, black market is expensive, and our parents could not pay the same for each of their children that they had paid for me. At school I tried to be as discreet as possible.

At this time, people did not realize the enormous expansion of the Japanese. They were even occupying the Aleutian Islands. People did not understand the importance of the victory of U.S. aircraft carriers in the Coral Sea, in the area of Midland Island, which meant that the Japanese could no longer invade Australia. In this month of May, which should have been given to the joy of the return of spring, the attention went to the order that Jews wear a yellow star sewn on their clothes. We could not know what would be the consequences of such a strange command.

Our father had had me work the sunniest part of the small garden by our house in Montreuil-sous-bois, and had planted seeds of tomato. Every evening he worked in our basement to build strange, wooden boxes, two feet by two feet by two feet. Then he painted them white and told us that they were bee hives to provide honey to our family in Hambye. One Sunday, he requested Philip and me walk with him to the paint factory where he was employed. There we found a handcart, where we put three big earthen jugs each three feet high. Thanks to the cart, we brought these jugs to our house. We were careful to return the cart on the same day.

I made a short trip to Le Havre, as they had invited me. On arrival at the railway station, I saw no one waiting for me. I went into the hall. Suddenly, a man jumped in front of me: "Quick! I must not be seen."

It was one of my cousins Daligault, who was a navy officer. We ran to a car belonging to the Ateliers Doré. He drove me to 75, Francis the First Boulevard, telling me that, as nobody was available, he had agreed to take care of me. He apologized that he had to get quickly to a less visible spot.

Gabrielle opened the door for me. She apologized also, saying that she had got only a short holiday, and led me to the red bedroom. One pane of glass on one of the two windows had been replaced by a piece of plywood.

"We are no longer replacing panes of glass by panes of glass. We are using plywood, as it does not break during bombing. It gives work to the Ateliers," she finished with a smile.

It was a dark day with a low sky. It added to a feeling of abandonment in the house. Theresa was no longer here and I got no information about her happenings. The meal was served as usual in the dark dining room on a white sheet covering the large table. The only people around it were my grandmother, Gabrielle, her elder sister Lalen, and me. There was barely any conversation.

The following morning Gabrielle woke me up and told me to rush. Gabrielle's brother Francis was waiting for us in a car from the Ateliers. From time to time there was a shower, but it was a short trip to get to Les Hellandes. There, Francis, limping as usual, followed by Gabrielle, went to the gardener's house. Both came back their arms full of splendid vegetables; the gardener brought to the car lots of eggs and milk from the two cows of my grandmother. There was no conversation, as it was urgent to be back home before the inspectors would start to harass people.

There was no other event during my short stay. Gabrielle took care of me as usual. My grandmother did not say much, and Lalen even less.

On July 13, our father, Philip, and I were back in Hambye. We brought the bee hives on the back of a horse carriage, as well as the bicycle our father was using between the house and the railway station when he was alone. On the following day, our father showed me a stone looking like solid mercury.

"This is a piece of galena," he told me. "Let's get up to the attic with this material."

He collected what he had put on the table and I followed him. On a piece of wood of about two feet by one foot, he screwed two or three instruments and fixed a couple of receivers to one of them.

"Put that on," he told me, showing the receivers. "Now take this wire and touch the galena with its end. Do you hear something?"

"No," I replied.

"Try another spot," he told me.

There was a faint sound.

"Try until you get a good sound."

After seven or eight attempts I got a clear voice, which I recognized to be one from the BBC. Our father made a number of adjustments.

"Now we need an antenna, that the Germans cannot see. It has to be long, as we are not using power."

Our father looked around for a moment. Then he arrived at a decision: "This is the best."

"But this is their telephone line!"

"It is very long and therefore excellent. And we shall not have to hide it."

He connected the telephone line to our galena set. It worked wonderfully. I just had to hide the connecting wire and the set itself. If the Germans discovered what we had done, they would shoot me, as our father had no intention to use the set.

Our father left the attic. As I had not heard the BBC for some weeks, I could not stop listening to it now. Again it was speaking about the many ships which were sunk. It did not indicate how many lives had been lost at sea. . . .

Our father was busy the next days getting swarms of bees for the hives he had installed in the bottom of the garden. His hope was to supplement with honey the little ration of sugar our family was getting. The family was a little afraid of getting bitten. It was certain that no one would volunteer to collect honey at the time.

A few days later, I heard that on July 22 the pro-German officials of Paris had arrested twenty-two thousand Jews for no reason except that they were Jews. It was now forbidden for Jews in France to enter into a public building!

Germans had been stopped in front of Leningrad and in front of Moscow, but reached Stalingrad on the Volga River and were attacking in the direction of the oil fields in the Caucasus. Some people pretended that if they would get to the Turkish border, Turkey would join them against the Soviet Union. The truth is that Soviets were leaving nothing to the Germans. They had moved their industries to the east and had destroyed everything which could be of help to the Germans. The front line was so extended that it was now even easier for the guerillas to get into the German lines and attack their transportation.

It became very hot in August. We discovered Colorado beetles among our potatoes. At first we tried to remove them one by one, as we had no pesticide. Then our father told our mother to do as he did in his small garden: collect cigarette ends and put them in water for at least one night. The following day, this water worked very well as an insecticide.

An immense hope spread among all of us on August 19, 1942, when it was announced that Canadian Rangers had landed in Dieppe at dawn. We were surprised that such a difficult place had been chosen: a cliff full of machine guns. It was with great sadness that we heard that before noon the surviving soldiers had re-embarked. Not only that—it had not been the great landing we were all hoping for, and we discovered that the German air force was still alive and could inflict bad losses. The pro-Germans were triumphant. They should have looked to Africa and to the east. Germans were short of gas and the Allies were bombing their manufacturers.

However, August was a wonderful time for us children. Looloo, the other eldest sister of our mother, had sent her five children to Hambye. We were glad to have our cousins with us. We played a lot together. As the roads were empty during the day, the eldest ones of us were going everywhere on their bikes; they explored each town around; they grew especially fond of Montmartin. It was a long beach of soft sand. To arrive at it, we had to get past sand hills covered by plants not adverse to salt. Barbed wire forbade getting on them, except for a lane. On each side of the line, there was a wooden board with the words *Achtung Minen* ("Keep out! Mines"). There was no danger of going where the mines were hidden, as on each side of the lane barbed wire ensured we walked only where it was safe. We followed the lane with our bikes and stopped on the beach.

The first time we went to this beach, the sky was low, the sea dead, both the color of steel. On the left lay the swollen corpse of a German sailor. We gave it a look and quickly moved to the water. It was tepid, agreeable. For a couple of hours we ran and swam in it, happy to have discovered this beach so near our house. Later, thanks to our bikes, we visited it often. One day the corpse had been removed. Was it the sea that had retaken it, or was it people who would have given it a funeral?

Another sister of our mother had arrived with her husband for a few days. Guite and Bernard loved to walk. We showed them the road to Mauny. On the way, there was a farm where three big dogs barked as loudly as they could. The farmer there had decided not to wait for the end of the war in a prison camp and had escaped. Wherever he went, a fourth big dog accompanied him. He was happy to be able to take care of his farm and be with his wife. In case of unwanted visitors, he could hide quickly. You could not meet his wife at church, as she was careful not to utter dangerous words.

Along the road to Mauny, we went by the ruins of an ancient castle from the time when Normandy was independent. On the side of the hill there had been a quarry. Pèdro and Alfonso, the two Spaniards who used to work there, had vanished in 1940.

The old stone bridge upon the Sienne River was at the center of a wooded valley. A bomb aimed at it had fallen on the house of a miller. It had been lucky that his mother did not move out of her bed, as the bomb had destroyed part of their house up to the place of the bed. The miller had saved his mother, but had not taken the bed away. We could see it from the road.

Gabrielle, Taee, and Vev spent also a few days in Hambye. We were pleased to see them seated for long periods of time on the bench near the door, helping our mother with vegetables or just chatting. No one knew about their activities and we did not ask. We were without news from Theresa.

Our paternal grandfather preferred to stay in his house in Laval, attended by his maid, visited from time to time by our father.

Once a month our father came to Hambye. Usually we children tried not to meet him too much. However, one day a small car stopped by our gate and a lean, black-haired man in a two-piece grey suit entered. Our father happened to be in the garden and the man started a long interrogation of him. After the man had left, I asked my father, "Why did you not invite this man in?" (Such was the custom.)

"He was from the prefecture and was looking for information on Jews in the area."

The following visit of our father was not so pleasant. An unknown woman had accused our sister Juliet to be wanting in respect toward her. Our father ordered Juliet to get down to the basement. Instead of that, Juliet ran away as fast as she could. We were shouting that the woman was lying. But our father ran after Juliet, took her to the basement, and a moment later we could see that Juliet was suffering and had tears in her eyes.

The following day, we were many in the dining room for the lunch when our father ordered me to go to the basement. I did not know his cause. As I knew I could not escape from him, I went down. I tried to remain silent, but I had a lot of pain. I went up to my bedroom and went to bed. It was difficult not to cry, and I wondered if one day I could get away from him. When I was much younger, Gabriel had given me a book that told the story of a boy who had run away from his harsh parents. I had not heard the light steps of Vev. She went up to me and gave me a big kiss. It was all I needed not to feel desperate. When our paternal grandfather was in Hambye, our father did not hurt us.

In Hambye, Philip visited his friends and they liked to see him because his gaiety, his humor, and his care.

Our mother trusted Mireille, the maid she had in 1942. She entrusted her with her five younger children and the house, and went to Montreuil-sous-bois for a few days to see how things were. One afternoon she took me to the largest menswear store in Vincennes with all her coupons for clothes. There was enough to buy a two-piece costume for me, but not enough to buy even pants for Philip. I felt ashamed.

Two in our class wore yellow stars sewn on their clothes this month of October: Beer and Bramnick. We looked at them with a mixture of anger, curiosity, and compassion. They were young like us. Why did they have to be discriminated against, allowed to use only the last car of a subway train and forced to get up from their seat every time a German appeared? We suspected that worse was waiting for them. As a matter of fact, two days later they stopped attending classes.

Philip had chosen to learn German. Was it because of Mrs. Lahr, who was from Luxembourg? We continued to learn nothing in our classes in English. In general, our new teachers were inferior to those we had the previous year. But we continued to enjoy good time in the Père Lachaise Cemetery for each air raid alert.

November 1942 brought plenty of hope. On November 2, the Eighth Army of General Bernard Montgomery had routed General Rommel and his men at El Alamein. On November 7, U.S. troops led by General Dwight D. Eisenhower landed in Morocco and in Algeria. Admiral François Darlan, the governor appointed by Pétain, ordered his men not to shoot on the Allies. Some of these soldiers enlisted in the French 2nd Armored Division, arriving from central Africa. A few days later, a criminal assassinated Darlan. But in May 1943, the last Germans and Italians in Africa would surrender. Afraid to be sent to Russia, looking for safety and good food, more than three hundred and fifty thousand Germans and Italians would be made prisoners. The blockade of Malta ended.

On November 19, General Georgy Zhukov, who had read the books of the German general, Heinz Guderian, and studied his victory of 1940 in western Europe, and his new T-34 had started a move of eight hundred kilometers westward. The Germans, who no longer had enough troops on their rear, were unable to stop him. They were trying to encircle Stalingrad, but now they were themselves encircled, deprived from the support of their commissariat.

Germans had hoped to capture the French fleet in Toulon. The sailors of this fleet wished to join the Allies. On November 27, the officers of this fleet again took the stupid and cruel decision of scuttling it.

The end of the German surface fleet was going to happen soon. On December 31, 1942, in the Barentz Sea, two German heavy cruisers and six German destroyers routed fourteen Allied merchant ships on their way to Russia. But the Allied escort ships severely damaged the two cruisers. Hitler decided that his surface warships were obsolete. The "great admiral" Erich Raeder, who had opposed the invasion of Russia and still had faith in his surface war vessels, resigned in May 1943, replaced by the head of the submarine fleet, Karl Dönitz. Germany now understood what the United States had known since Pearl Harbor: that battleships and heavy cruisers belonged to the past. But Germany did not have the capacity to build the aircraft carriers, which would provide victories for the United States.

In Montreuil-sous-bois, the winter was harder and harder on us. We got one hundred kilos of coal with our coupons, and we were saving them for the coldest days. From time to time our father burned books of a large classical collection he had inherited. It was not much heat, but we were pleased to see and feel the flames.

Now we started to understand why our father had brought with our help those three big jars. He had hidden them under the basement stairway and filled two of them with strawberry jam and the third one with salicilat. Little by little, he added dozens of eggs to the salicilat. This provision of jam and eggs gave us a security we did not have before. Very often our father was in Laval to help his father get wood and food, and in Le Mans to get food for his brother.

We were happy, Philip and I, to be back to Hambye for a couple of weeks. We learned that three hundred workers from Cherbourg naval dockyards had been sent to Kiel to build submarines for the Germans. It was surprising to see how our younger sisters and brothers had changed. Juliet had become tall and still had beautiful red hair; Arlette, Geofroy, Gilles, and Clovis were now taking care of themselves and were also, in many ways, helping our mother.

The Germans had allowed a few prisoners to get back to their farms. Women had celebrated their return with joy. But many more were still in camps, and now the recruitment of manpower to send to Germany was more and more feared.

11
Preface

In Hambye, German soldiers did not stop to tell us how frightened they were of being sent to Russia. They no longer believed in what was being told to them, and they were asking us what we had learned. In Russia, news for them grew worse and worse.

We were getting more and more details through Philip, who had started to learn German at school. The soldiers in charge of the tank near our house, had become fond of him and invited him to visit their tank, and were showing him how to operate it. They also told him that they were allowed only fifty liters of gas per day. Philip discovered that they were hiding a supplement of gas in a bush at about ten meters from their tank. Philip was told that German soldiers did not like receiving coffee and "schnapps" as it meant that they were going to fight.

First there was the winter. They were still not well equipped to face it. Another fear came from the guerillas. The front was too long and Soviets were getting through their lines without being detected. The German tactics of terror were now working against them, as they had raised the whole population against them.

On January 11, 1943, twenty-one thousand guns, fifteen hundred Katyusha rocket-launchers, and six hundred antiaircraft guns started a massive fire against German lines around Leningrad. After a siege of eight hundred sixty-five days by the Germans, the Russians in the city were in poor health. They suffered from hunger, cold, and sicknesses. But Lieutenant-General Leonid Govorov, after an intense bombing of seven days and the support of over one million men, took back Shlisselburg and broke the blockade around Leningrad.

To the west of Stalingrad, the move of General Zhukov was successful. Three hundred and thirty thousand Germans, surrounded, lacking food and munitions, surrendered. On February 8, the Russians were back in Rostov; on February 16, in Kharkov.

From Hambye, we were told that on February 6 the Todt Organization had evacuated three hundred of its Russian slaves from the Channel Islands; emaciated, grey, without shoes, they were put on cattle cars in Cherbourg and sent to Germany.

The planes arriving from North America with their crews, their passengers, and their goods were increasing every day the air power of the Allies in the West. They had enlarged their control over the Mediterranea and increased their bombings over Germany.

I spent a few days in Le Havre. During my stay, a Spanish ship brought a cargo of oranges to the city. People were so pleased. My uncle Francis arrived at the house of my grandmother with a big bag and shared with other families in the area. One evening I arrived at Saint-Lazare Station in Paris. There were inspectors by the engine.

"Stop! Open your suitcase."

I stopped, but did not open my suitcase.

"If you wish to open my suitcase, do it yourself," I said.

One of the inspectors took my suitcase and put it on his knees. It was not difficult for him to open it. But all of a sudden two dozens of oranges ran into every direction, some under the engine.

"I would like my oranges back in my suitcase," I said.

The inspector and another one went all over collecting my oranges. When they had finished and locked my suitcase, all the other passengers were gone. . . .

Philip, our father, and Mrs. Lahr were so happy to get some oranges the next days, a fruit they had not seen for a long time.

The great tragedies continued on the seas, in the bombed cities, and on the fronts. At school we had a strange feeling of normality. Classes were held regularly. Mr. Andrieu gave us a solid course in French, Latin, and Greek. The English teacher continued, like his predecessors, not to teach English seriously. Philip and I were pleased to spend a few days in Le Havre at Easter. There were few people to pay attention to us, but we enjoyed long walks along the coast with the bunkers on one side and the harbor on the other. We were especially pleased that we could get on the dam. Inside, the harbor looked more like a historical curiosity than a modern facility, as there were no ships. At home, Philip and I had long games of Monopoly in the hall. Before our departure, our grandmother told us that she could no longer invite us, as bombings were becoming more frequent and more dangerous. We did not take that sadly. We knew our grandmother loved us. To us, what she meant was that a landing was in preparation. An important harbor such as Le Havre would be disputed between the Allies and the Germans. The end of the war was coming near.

With the rising temperature of the air, studying was becoming less hard. Mr. Puget was teaching us about light, which supposed demonstrations in the obscurity. We were posted at different points of the laboratory and Mr. Puget was manipulating light rays. We had to follow.

A teacher should not immerse himself with his class in obscurity. As soon as the power was off, we heard from various parts of the laboratory calls of, "Here, the Pupu! Here the Pupu!" But Mr. Puget remained impassive and we had enjoyed our moment of anarchy.

In April, there were such nice afternoons that we opened the windows. A football flew inside our classroom on the first floor. Martin gave up his translation of Cicero, got up, and sent the ball back to the courtyard. The ball went back through one of our open windows. Before it got to the floor, Martin had already caught it up and sent it back. The ball flew back.

"Martin, sit down," said Mr. Andrieu.

"I cannot, sir," replied Martin. "They are sending the ball."

Right at this time the ball flew again into the classroom.

"Send this ball back, close the window, and return to your seat," said Mr. Andrieu.

We were not happy to have the windows closed, but Martin brought to a close his translation of Cicero, this republican lawyer full of angriness against the corrupt administrators of Sicily. . . .

With each new day of May, girls were becoming more beautiful. It was amazing to observe how easily they walked on their wood soles fixed with cardboard lashes. Their hair was falling on their shoulders and a breeze made their light spring dresses undulate. It did not appear to us, but they too were hungry.

At the scouts, one of the other boys told me confidentially, "Next year, we shall be taught the handling of weapons."

I did not reply. Germans were killing ten hostages for each of them killed. The true resisters were not killing Germans. What they were doing was sabotage, especially on railway tracks, as Germans were short of gas for their vehicles. One day they would do much more, disrupting the German armed forces.

THE FIVE SISTERS

In the small garden of Montreuil-sous-bois, defended by its iron gate, we could now see some yellow flowers on the tomato plants, some small lettuces, and the young stems of potatoes. They would help our father to eat when he no longer made his short trips to Hambye, Laval, or Le Mans, and continue instead to work at his paint factory.

12

A Cupboard Bottom

Our father was a devoted man. But Philip and I would have preferred not to live with him in Montreuil-sous-bois. At the end of every week he requested each of us, one after the other, to get downstairs to the basement. There we were ordered to remove our pants and he whipped us with a lash. When Mrs. Lahr was still in our house, she requested that he not beat us. He just waited for her to finish her work and depart. Then he proceeded.

He had started to strike me when I was about six years old. As I felt ashamed, I did not speak about that to anyone. And it was a time when children were not supposed to speak to grown-ups unless having been asked to. On Monday mornings at school, I could not stay seated. I had too much pain. Miss Henriette, the teacher, then sent me to a corner of the room. Standing up was allowing me to suffer less. It usually took three or four days for me to feel comfortable again.

At other times, our father slapped my face. I knew when it was going to happen. There was a certain nervousness in the corner of his eye and on the side of his hand. At other times, he repeated to me that I was a flabby fellow. When Philip got near the age of six years old, our father started to treat him the same. Later, our sister Juliet, then our sister Arlette. As Arlette was depressive, it caused her tears for long hours and our father dubbed her "the squalling brat."

When our brother Geoffroy was near his six years of age, our mother ordered to our father, "No! Not this one."

Geoffroy was never beaten. Why? We did not know, we children. Today, I believe I have the answer.

Gilles and Clovis were also badly treated, just the same as Philip, Juliet, Arlette, and I.

It was strange to us that it seemed that other children were not beaten. We were not bad children; on the contrary. We could not understand the behavior of our father.

Many parents used terms of endearment with their own children. Our parents did not. It was our grandmothers, our aunts, some of our maids who used kind words for us. Our teachers were always polite with us.

The family of our mother was not a violent one. Why did not she stop our father? Mrs. Lahr did all she could to have him behave.

Today I think that our mother, with her seven children, was fully dependent on our father for a living. But was that the only explanation?

There was a kind of patriotism in not being violent. We felt like civilized people in the face of Germans. Along the coast, we used to hear their noncommissioned officers call their subordinates *Schweinkopf* ("pig head").

It was in January 1943. Philip, our father, and I were in Montreuil-sous-bois at the time. A wet snow was falling from the sky. I felt that I could no longer accept to be insulted and to be beaten. I took my warmest clothes and a little to eat. Philip was busy upstairs. I did not even say good-bye to him: I needed all the strength of my resolution. I opened silently the street door and left. Brokenhearted, I walked towards the subway station we used to get to Voltaire high school, "Croix-de-Chavaux." I knew I could get some heat in the subway. I went to another station, sat there for hours, and then to another where I did the same; then to the station "Château de Vincennes" where I sat until an employee announced that the subway would be closed for the night. I left. It was night, but not as dark as night by the coast. I could see the fortress on my left. There was nobody outside. I was tired and hungry. Not knowing what to do, I walked to a stone bench and sat on it. Everything was quiet. Finally I decided to lie down on the bench. It was cold, but I knew that in five or six hours I could get again into the subway.

I slept. When I woke up, I was feeling very cold. But happily the subway was open, and I spent the day there until closing time. I spent the night on the same bench. After warming up in the subway for several hours, I decided that I could not continue as I was. A fellow student was living not very far and I walked to the house of his parents, the Vanzons. They were both home and they invited me to come in and warm up a little. I explained my situation. After a while, they arrived at the conclusion that I had to get back to the house of my parents. I was not ready to accept it, but what could I do? To register to work in Germany? They did not see another alternative. Mrs. Vanzon went to speak to our father, who was eager to have me back. A few hours later, at the beginning of the night, afraid of being heavily beaten, I rang at the door of my father.

He opened silently the door and made me go to the dining room. Philip was there and we exchanged a glance. I knew that he understood. Our father kept silent. I was waiting for the punishment. Each of us was standing. Two meters were separating us. At last, our father said, "You made us afraid. I could not go to the police. I forbid you from speaking to your brothers and sisters." Then he withdrew in the drawing room. I was very hungry, but decided to wait for the diner.

Of course he could not prevent me from speaking with Philip when he was away. Days went by: our father showed angriness towards me, but he had stopped beating me. Alas, he had not stopped with my brothers and sisters. As for our mother, she did not comment to me on the situation the next time we met. She seemed not to care about the beatings dealt out by of our father.

They were years of violence.

13

Hope

The traditional road of the British to India and Hong Kong was through Gibraltar, Malta, the Suez Canal, and Singapore. The Allies had re-conquered the southern shore of the Mediterranean and their airplanes were getting dominance over the whole area. This made it easier for the British fleet to combine with the new powerful Pacific fleet of the United States. Now it was time to recapture the territories lost in the east. Most people around us did not understand this aspect of the war.

Philip and I were now back to Montreuil-sous-bois. Cooking was more and more difficult and dangerous. As there was less and less pressure, more and more often the fire on gas died out; now, when the pressure came back, gas diffused in the kitchens. If you were not careful, you could provoke an explosion.

It was wonderful how well the subway was operating. It was a great resource for everybody.

Usually, three times a week, the first person we saw arriving from the first train was our neighbor the grocer. Contrary to his colleagues, he did not wait for the authorities to bring food to his store. He went through the country and brought what he could find for his customers in a big bag he was carrying on a shoulder.

As he was a cheerful man, he made friends easily and was always ready to help. He traded food, wine, and cigarettes for rare goods such as soap, butter, cognac, or even wine. He could sell what you needed for a high price.

Each year there was construction around his store. He used beautiful red bricks to build rooms for tenants, and each year he added one floor. Renting at current fares, his temperament made him liked by his tenants.

On the other side of the street, one or two times a year, a German soldier visited his sister, who had married a Frenchman before the war. She had a store of wools in Vincennes, but did not sell much in those days. Neighbors did not consider her an enemy and were friendly to her. But this year she decided to move to another country for a while, to be safe.

In the subway there were now many posters promoting the idea of "Europa."

One day, one of my classmates and I were waiting for the next train, when I said, "Who cares about this posters?"

"If you wish to enlist in the Legion of the French Volunteers and fight in Russia for the Germans," replied Grimbert.

"Some do," I said.

"If you wish to escape from the compulsory work service and get good food," observed Grimbert, "but you may lose a leg or more, and not be welcome back."

It was clear that none of us was ready to enlist in the LVF, and that we did not understood those who did.

The two of our fellow students who were the thinnest had given up their studies. For what? We did not know.

It was poignant to see hungry young women. Mothers were getting supplements, but it was not enough. When they could, they moved to a farm. As for white heads, they had almost disappeared.

We had a bright geography teacher. He presented us maps without words, and by studying the geology, the relief, the waters, and the climate we had to find where people were and what they were doing. Martin was happy to participate in exercises in the chemistry laboratory. In December he combined retorts, pipes, bottles, pipettes, and all the materials he could assemble into a huge construction of different liquids and powders. He was so proud of what he had done that he started a dance around the laboratory, when all of sudden we heard a big explosion. Happily, Martin was far from his masterpiece. As he was usually a quite good student, he got only reprimanded.

Christmas in Hambye was again a good time around our mother, in warm rooms with plenty to eat. As before, January and February in Montreuil-sous-bois were a hard time. In March, more and more often, the temperature went above ten degrees and it was a joy to feel the spring coming. Finding food was becoming even more difficult. The bread turned yellow as more and more corn flour was added to bake it.

One evening we heard big bangs on the door. Two Gestapo policemen entered into the house. They spoke only German and made us understand that there were some rays of light coming from our house. Our father arrived and expressed himself in German, softening the two men. In fact both were afraid, as they were in an area never visited by Germans, except by the brother of our neighbor.

A few days after Philip and I had come back to Hambye, we heard that on July 10, 1943, the Allies had landed in Sicily. Soon it appeared that it was not a new Dieppe and that the Allies were going to conquer Sicily.

In Hambye the bread had not changed and continued to be good. A farmer had given the authorization to glean on his fields. The quantity of ears of wheat harvested by our younger sisters and brothers was astonishing. The grain was separated. Part of it was exchanged for flour at the mill of Hambye. The other part was crushed in our coffee mills and mixed with eggs and milk, giving us a kind of good cake.

One evening when it was already dark, not telling anyone, Philip left the house and walked to the school. There the Germans were stocking clothes. A couple of hours later, Philip came back and gave our mother five green great-coats. Surprised, happy, she was overjoyed. Philip did not explain how he had got the clothes. He just said that he had seen them being thrown out from a basement window.

The next morning, hiding from the Germans in the house, we quickly removed the identifications and put them in the fire of the kitchen stove. In a remote corner of the drawing room our mother separated with her scissors the different parts. She sent me to the borough haberdasher to buy navy blue dye and Philip far away into the fields in case the Germans tried to get him and punish him.

Soon the canvasses had taken the new color. Our mother sent Louise, her second maid, to have them dry in the attic as our mother was afraid of the neighbors. A couple of days later, our mother invited separately the two neighboring farmers' wives and gave each of them enough to make a pair of pants. She gave something to her two maids and was careful not to give any explanation. The women were pleased and would not speak.

The first pair of pants went to Philip. Then our mother made some for me and different clothes for the family. Germans continued to circulate in the kitchen and use the stove of our mother for themselves. Apparently they saw nothing.

We happened to learn that shoes with cord soles were sold in a store in the neighboring borough of Saint-Denis-le-Gast. The following afternoon our mother led her seven children to this store. Yes, they had such shoes for sale. We saw them. They did not look of good quality. But our need was such that our mother bought eight pairs of these shoes, one for her and one for each of her children.

The shoes were comfortable but fragile. However, to repair the soles, we found that we could use the liquid tar of the road.

As I was listening to the BBC one afternoon, I heard the noise of boots in the stairway to the attic. I quickly threw a blanket over the radio set and started purling onions. An officer and a soldier appeared. Without salutation they stopped at the door, looking in every direction. A wire remained visible. I did not direct my attention in its direction. After a while the two men left. I left too, and for a couple of days I stayed far from the house.

At the end of August, British, Americans, and Canadians were holding Sicily. At this time, two German officers told my parents that they needed a bedroom. They visited the whole house and declared that the room they wished was our parents' bedroom.

"But there is only a double bed," said my mother.

"This is exactly what we want," said one of the officers.

Walking on a secondary road, I heard the motor of an airplane just in time to jump in a ditch. The airplane arrived very near. I heard the machine gun. Then it went. I verified that it was not coming back and then looked at the road. Where I was walking there were maybe twenty holes. I said, "Thank you, God, for having saved my life."

My tasks in Hambye remained the same and gave me the feeling of being useful. Philip was doing more and more, Juliet was asking questions about what she could do, and from time to time was given small tasks.

Gabrielle, Taee, Ver and Theresa had spent two weeks in Hambye as every summer. It was such a pleasure for all of us. And we could see too that they appreciated all the food our mother was offering them, happy to have them around.

At the end of August, British, Americans, Canadians, Poles, and French were holding Sicily. Germans sent against them some of their soldiers who could be quite dangerous. But they could not stop the Allies' determination, now that they had enough of their own soldiers and enough planes and ships to back them. In September they landed in continental Italy. Mountains made their conquest slow.

The "Germans" we had then in Hambye were not Germans. They were mostly Rumanians, heavy men in their fifties, a bit slow. They seemed to spend much time in the washroom, which was inconvenient to us.

October was approaching. Our parents were afraid to send Philip and me back by train. More and more trains were machine-gunned by airplanes; rail sabotages were becoming more and more frequent. The opportunity appeared to them to send us on a truck. During the obscurity roads were safe. Germans knew that it was a condition they could use to move their tanks, their guns, their trucks, and their cars.

Thus on the first evening of October 1943, a horse carriage took Philip and me to a door in a long wall in Villedieu-les-Poêles, twenty-four kilometers from our house in Hambye. Inside the wall, men were loading a truck with ox carcasses for the provisioning of Paris. We were told to wait. They put in the middle of the truck a cabin of boards with spaces between and with a couple of chairs. We got in. The men put additional carcasses between the cabin and the edge of the truck. We were told not to speak when the truck stopped. We went.

It was completely dark in the cabin. But we were feeling safe, as if a plane could attack us and the meat would protect us. There was little smell, so it was not too unpleasant.

Three hundred kilometers later the truck stopped. We were hearing dogs. One by one the carcasses were removed and we could leave. Tall Danes were jumping around, but not aggressively. We were in a small yard. Men were hanging the carcasses in a well-lighted building. The passive defense could not see this light from the street, but it was certainly visible from the sky. We were pleased to leave and reach the subway, which had just opened its doors.

One more school year at Voltaire high school! It was good to meet again the same students. We did not ask questions about the summer of our fellow students. It was private and could be dangerous.

To our surprise, we had for our physics teacher a woman, and not just any woman. She was in her twenties and very pretty. We were fifteen or sixteen years of age. We were delighted.

The course started normally. But as soon as the teacher started to write on the blackboard, a few cries burst out.

"Darling!"

"Beauty!"

"Love!"

She stopped writing and looked at us. We remained silent. She wrote again on the blackboard and we heard similar cries. She stopped again. It was silent again. During the whole hour of teaching, as soon as she could not see us she could hear those of us who were calling to her.

The next time she taught us it was the same. And the third time too. She cried. Her face was full of tears, which made her even more beautiful. She left and never came back.

Because of a second reform of the programs in three years, we were taught for the third time the history of the French Revolution and of Napoleon. Our two preceding teachers had had the pleasure to describe to us the miseries of the "Great Army" in the cold of Russia, the battle of Borodino to cool the most excited Russian military, the guerillas making difficult the provisioning of Napoleon's soldiers and putting Moscow to fire, the retreat of Napoleon and the impossibility of his whole army to get across the Berezina River . . . of course, they never made any reference to the Germans in Russia.

Philip was not happy in Voltaire high school. He had been interested a little in studying German and some mathematics. But our father did not understand that Philip was very good with his hands, just like his grandfather and his great-grandfather who had created the Ateliers Doré. Philip made different objects, including a miniature tank, with care and precision. He should have been trained as a cabinetmaker. But for our father and for a number of teachers, people working with their hands were inferior, even if some acquired a large fortune. They felt you had to have achieved at least grade thirteen to be recognized. Our mother did not seem to understand that Philip was wasting his time in a high school. Mrs. Lahr, the widow of a carpenter, knew what was wrong with the education of Philip, but our father pretended not to care about the opinions of someone who had not graduated university. Philip liked to spend time near Mrs. Lahr, who seemed to understand him. In Hambye he was happy with farmers' offspring.

The eggs and the strawberry jam saved by our father in his house, the butter, the meat, and the "milk jam" of our mother were of a great help in Montreuil-sous-bois. After a two-week period eating rutabagas, we spent a week eating Jerusalem artichokes before eating rutabaga again. We could get bread for our coupons, a bread which included over time more and more sawdust; it was prudent to remove the splinters before eating. Coupons for other edibles were useless. Stores were mostly empty. However, as with other adults, our father got coupons for wine and for cigarettes still on sale, and he exchanged part of these for food. He also used his soap to get some. But it was not enough. Soon our father was burning again a few books to get some heat.

The events in Italy were confusing to us. This country had signed an armistice. The Italian fleet was no longer part of the battle. Marshal Pietro Badoglio was trying to establish peace. But fanatical German soldiers were stopping the Allies.

We were waiting for the winter, as we believed that it would be the time for the Soviets to re-conquer Russia.

When Christmas arrived, it was decided that we would again use trains to get to Hambye. We knew of no other alternative. As in every year, we were glad to get back. The happiest was Philip. I was tried to make myself useful to our mother, but I did not have the feeling to belong to her family. Senlis, Agneaux, Le Fayet, Montreuil-sous-bois, even Le Havre had separated my life from that of our sisters and brothers. I visited a few farmers, walked a lot. But few people spoke to me.

The Allies had heavily bombed the ramps for rockets, the naval dockyard, and the fortifications of Cherbourg. German soldiers in Normandy were older men. Younger men were coming. Here and there they were digging trenches. At the time of battle, they would get coffee and brandy, which they were not used to getting. But by night, resisters moved signposts to different places along the roads, causing Germans to get lost.

Back in Montreuil-sous-bois, we learned that they were again requisitioning horses, which obliged farmers to hide theirs. On February 11, 1944, came the unpleasant news that three-quarters of the trains had been suppressed.

But on February 29, we heard that there was again a French navy as three French destroyers sunk a German frigate and a German sloop of war. The Russians were now routing the Germans on the Dniepr and Dniestr Rivers.

In Montreuil-sous-bois, it was more and more difficult to cook something as the gas pressure was very low. One day around noon I told Philip, "It is nice. We have now warm water."

"It cannot be," answered Philip. "But, yes, you are right."

"It is curious. What can cause that?"

"It is better to check in the basement," observed Philip. He went down and came back. "There is a fire!"

I joined him. A blue flame was making the pipe melt. He rushed to get a plumber. The man did the repair and explained to us that because of the low gas pressure the fire had gone down into the pipe. One more time, our lunch was cold.

Little by little, the temperature was getting better, the days longer. In the night of April 18-19, 1944, British airplanes bombed the railway complex of Rouen, causing eight hundred deaths. Bakers become short of flour. We had to visit two or three times "our" baker to be able to get bread for our coupons. Even rutabagas and Jerusalem artichokes began to get scarce. One beautiful sunny day, Philip said, "We have to do something. I know where there are many dandelions."

We took the largest bags we could and knives and went to Vincennes. We bypassed the fortress and started to walk in the wood until we arrived at the barracks' railway track. Philip was right. There were plenty of superb dandelions showing their beautiful yellow flowers to the sky. As the area did not attract people, we were sure that these plants were clean. We cut as many as we could to fill our bags and went back home. For three days we ate these dandelions, as there was little else aside the eggs and the jam.

On May 17, 1944, the Poles captured Calvario at Cassino; then the French Garigliano. It was the Allied victory that opened the road to Rome, captured on June 4. All along the way, the Poles who had been integrated forcibly in the German army were rejoining the Polish forces.

In the beginning of June, British planes bombed Rouen again.

As war was expanding towards Germany itself, our parents decided that it was no longer the time to stay in the Paris area. Philip, our father, and I were lucky to board the last train from Saint-Lazare Station to Granville. Usually we boarded the trains to Granville in Montparnasse Station.

The train was crowded. Like many other passengers, we had no seat but our small cardboard suitcase. The train did not seem to start. We waited for one hour, two hours. At last it left Saint-Lazare Station. No one had said anything. Normans are quiet people.

For awhile our train went westward. Then it turned to the right. We were surprised, as it is the direction to Belgium. But it was known that there were many German trains and that bridges and switches had been destroyed. We were heading more and more to the north. Our father, Philip, and I were taking turns sitting on our small cardboard suitcase. People were looking at the names of the stations and continued to say little. At last, after a good couple of hours, our train turned to the left. We had crossed no river and our speed was not very fast. It was a relief to know that now we were riding westward.

14

Last Days

Philip and I were up by the large window of the car. He moved then towards me and said confidentially to me, "If there are no trains, there is no Voltaire high-school."

His face was beaming with a large smile. Our father had not heard him and was now opening our suitcase on the floor and distributing sandwiches to us. Everybody was already eating. We would have liked some water, but there was none. On the two sides of the tracks, we were seeing the many trees of the Norman country. Stations had familiar names: L'Aigle, Argentan . . . The sun was still high in the sky. We were arriving in Flers. The train had stopped when we heard an airplane and then a machine gun. All the passengers ran away as far as possible from the train. The plane was making a return. The engine exploded, probably killing its two drivers. Bullets penetrated the three first cars.

We sat for a while in the grass. The plane would probably not come back. The passengers were staying about thirty meters from the trains, waiting for the few who were trying to help people in the first cars or trying to get the suitcases they had abandoned. Rescue would soon come for the wounded.

"Our home is at about fifty kilometers," said our father.

This small old cardboard suitcase was full of soap, which was making it heavy. Our father had decided that alternatively each of us would carry this suitcase the distance between two electrical posts—my brother too! "We can cover this distance through walking for two days."

We got up, alternating the carrying of the suitcase. Philip did not say a word. He was courageous. At the end of the day, we had covered about twenty-two or twenty-three kilometers and were very thirsty. We approached a few houses.

"One of my uncles has a friend who is living here," said our father. "Maybe he would take care of us?"

We went to one of these grey houses with a slate roof and windows and doors painted white, as most houses in the area. Our father knocked at the door. After a while an old woman answered and our father explained the situation to her. She told us to wait and came back a few minutes later. We felt so happy!

Our granduncle's friend was a tall big man in his sixties, living alone with the help of the maid who had opened to us. He expressed neither pleasure nor boredom in meeting us. He only had his maid serve us a substantial vegetable soup, with lots of excellent country bread and milk. Then his maid led us to bedrooms, and soon I was in a bed with old but clean coarse sheets and an eiderdown. Our father woke me up. The three of us got a warm barley decoction with milk and, again, plenty of bread, this time with butter.

We did not spend much time thanking these people who had been so generous to us, as we still had two dozen kilometers to walk.

As we were nearing our house, plants and things were becoming familiar to us. Then we saw places we knew. There had been no planes in the sky in the whole day. We were so glad when we arrived home. Our mother was both surprised and happy. She was not sure we would come. We could wash ourselves, drink, and relax. Soon we were seated around a copious meal prepared in haste for us. Once in my bed, I slept immediately.

French policemen were hunting for young men to send to Germany to work for the Germans. The next day I went to Hambye city hall with my father to register for food coupons as new inhabitants in Hambye. The secretary, a light brown, young woman, told me to register for the compulsory work service: this way, she explained to me, the policemen would not be in too much of a hurry to catch me. She added that it would be even better if I would work for a farmer.

In the afternoon our father met with a neighboring farmer, René, and asked him if he would need some free help. It was difficult to get help on farms, and therefore René agreed immediately to sign a paper for the authorities. The following day I rushed on my bike to bring this paper to the secretary, who gave me a large smile.

I really liked to work as a farmhand for René. He and his wife Germaine, both blue-eyed and with a skin that the sun and the rain had colored red and brown, were excellent people. They had two sons: one called Gerard who was two years younger than me, one younger than him, and seven daughters. All loved their parents. Each child was trying his best to help.

Some of the work was repetitive, as animals need the same care every day. But soon you could see the appreciation of the animals when you treated them well. The hardest work was handling the heavy manure, but usually René himself took care of it. I loved to handle the hay as it smelled so good.

Every day was different on the farm, dictated by the weather. When there was little to do René sent me to help Germaine with the kitchen garden.

A number of tasks were collective. Neighbors helped neighbors collect apples and, later, make cider; harvest the hay and, when well-dried, store it; separate grains of wheat from the straw and collect both; and cut bushes and burn them. One day René had decided to cut his buckwheat. He was driving the mare drawing the mower. We could see them opening large paths among the red stems. Gerard, another boy of the same age as me, Grégoire, about a dozen women and girls, and I were all collecting the buckwheat stems in bunches. When René had finished cutting he left his mower and hid his mare far from the eyes of the Germans and the policemen. But the fun did not stop. Right from the beginning, everybody was making jokes and we were all laughing and laughing. And it was the same with the other tasks, except when they were noisy, such as when separating the grain from the stems.

Throughout the working day, Germaine or her two eldest daughters brought cider and buckwheat pancakes to the workers. In the evening we ate traditional cabbage soup with a little bit of pork and large slices of bread with plenty of butter.

Grégoire and I immediately agreed that we were not going to work for the Germans and that, when the time would become dangerous for us, we would hide together.

In the meantime our cousins had arrived. I could meet them only on Sundays, as the farm work was keeping me too busy on the other days. Philip had replaced me for the tasks I was performing for our mother and never complained. The cousins were also helping.

One day René came to our house and told our mother that he was going to kill one of his pigs. The following day he and his son Gérard brought a table, a number of pails of water, and kitchen material behind a hedge that could not be seen from the road. Then they captured with difficulty the biggest of René's pigs. The animal resisted as best he could. But finally René killed it. He and Gérard washed it with cold water and started to collect the blood. After they did their butchery. Each of the neighbors got a little piece of meat and some black pudding. No woman had attended, but each one was pleased by what they got. This is an aspect of farming I do not like too much. How much meat do we have the moral right to eat?

One Sunday, near the end of the afternoon, Philip, Juliet, our cousins, and I had a walk on the road. We were surprised to hear and then see five German armored cars coming. It was a dangerous time for them, as an airplane could easily gun them down. They stopped by us. There was no longer any reliable indication along the roads.

"Is the next main road to the left the way to Gavray?" asked an officer in a quite good French.

I suddenly got an unfriendly idea.

"Yes," I said. "You are right. But there is a shorter way. You see this lane in this field? Take it and you will arrive sooner."

"Merci, merci beaucoup," said the officer.

The five armored cars drove to the lane and continued on. It was true that the lane was a shorter way to Gavray, but only for pedestrians. Once on this cart track the cars found themselves on an increasing slope perpendicular to the lane. The first car began to roll along the slope; the second one followed it; the third one; the fourth one, and, at last, the fifth one. We rushed to hide ourselves. After a long while, as nothing seemed to happen, we got back on the road and walked home.

The city hall secretary gave a short warning to our parents on the telephone. I immediately got in touch with Grégoire, who was not long to arrive at our house with a small bag. I led him to an old bake house. René had brought much hay there. It was far from the road, with a complicated access among bushes. In addition to the door there was a window opening onto rear fences. Jumping from the window led to other bushes and to a little wood. Germans or policemen would be afraid of moving too deeply in this direction. We were going to get our food from my grandfather's house.

It was good time to hide. Two days later we saw two policemen on their bikes in the lane below us. They did not dare to get further. Like other French officials, they were not Normans and were afraid of penetrating deeper among the bushes and the fields.

At this time of the year the temperature was pleasant, even during the night. The hay smelled good and it was comfortable to sleep in it. I don't know how many days Grégoire and I would have been able to spend in the bake house. There was little to do for each of us.

15

Rescue Comes From the Sea (Old Norman Proverb)

May is so pretty in Normandy. Apple trees are white and pink. Calves, foals, and lambs play in the fields. May 1944 seemed to be the same, even though Allies were bombing stations and bridges. Farmers kept their young animals away from the roads, far from inspectors and thieves. Roads were deserted during the day, but full of German vehicles at night. As the headlights of cars were reduced to a small square, we could contemplate the moon and all the stars during the nights.

June seemed to be a beautifully warm and dangerous month, just like May. But in its very first days the sky became full of silvery airplanes coming from the sea. We were looking at them, so high they seemed motionless. Below these bombers were a few fighters. We knew that we had better not be visible to them.

We had heard that small submarines had set up on the beaches of Calvados, at the center of the Norman coast.

On June 6, 1944, early in the morning, radio informed us that paratroopers had been launched behind the Germans on the Norman coast. We got immediately excited. Was it a new Dieppe, or was it the landing we were all hoping for? We were also thinking that machine guns could easily kill a number of these courageous men during their jump, and that on the ground they would not be equipped with heavy weapons. On the other hand, we knew that many beaches were empty and that Germans were not prepared to fight an enemy coming from behind.

When on the same day the radio announced that tens of thousands U.S., British, Canadian, and other Allied soldiers were disembarking thanks to artificial harbors, we were sure that it was at last the rescue we had waited for so long. Bombers in the sky and destroyers from the sea had prepared the landings. They were occurring on beautiful sandy beaches in the area of Caen. They were called Sword, Juno, Gold, Omaha, and Utah. It was difficult to believe how many tanks, trucks, and other vehicles, as well as material victual ling and weaponry they were spreading on the sand. Soon the Regina Riffles and the First Hussars were occupying the borough of Courseulles.

Later that same day we were pleased to hear that the Gestapo had fled from Caen, but less pleased to hear that before departing they had killed the ninety guerillas they were holding in their jail.

In the evening we heard on the radio about heavy bombings on Norman cities: Caen, Saint-Lô, Falaise, Lisieux, Coutances, Périer, Isigny . . . thousands of people had been killed. Most who had been wounded were also dying, as the destructions prevented rescuing them and the hospitals themselves had been destroyed. The Allies had attempted to have civilians evacuate their cities. But few of their leaflets had reached them, blown by the wind, and people had not believed that the bombings would be so powerful. To them, their own basements would have been enough. Bombings of the cities continued for a week. Allies had been afraid of snipers in their buildings.

On June 12, the Allies had made their joining on the five beaches. Bayeux had been liberated on June 7. Despite bombing and gunning, Canadians and British were stopped in the area of Caen where the Germans could gun their positions. But the road to Carentan and Cherbourg, that is to say to the Cotentin, was opened to the Americans and it was a great opportunity.

Germans had become less visible. One afternoon at a crossroads I met the wife of a neighboring farmer.

"They are still around," she told me. "Just yesterday there were two of them in a car. Medical doctors. They were going from one weak . . . minded boarding house to another one, and injected into these people a poison to kill them."

Could that have been true? I was so shocked that I did not utter a word.

The Cotentin peninsula is about twenty-two kilometers wide, with a length of one hundred and ten kilometers for its western coast and twenty kilometers for its eastern one. In the past, Cotentin has been used a number of times as a stronghold, especially by the Vikings and by the Norman dukes. When in the fourteenth century the high constable Bertrand Du Guesclin was trying to conquer Normandy for the benefit of the king of France, he expelled all the inhabitants of Cotentin and destroyed their resources to make it difficult for their prince to come back. Cotentin is, indeed, a good military base for a conquest, and this both the Allies' supreme commander Dwight D. Eisenhower and the American General Omar N. Bradley believed.

The harbor of Cherbourg in Cotentin was deep enough for the largest ships. Many of the ships coming from North America could have used the smaller harbors of Saint-Vaast and Carentan. The area of the peninsula was necessary to spread troops and materiel, and would offer possibilities for airfields.

War was approaching Hambye, which lies to the south of Cotentin. Our parents were concerned by the bombing, so our father ordered Philip and me to dig a trench for the whole family. We did not spend much time digging one, as we too were afraid. We covered it with logs and earth. Some farmers did the same for themselves and their families, but not all of them.

After completion of the trench, our father ordered me to dig a hole of three meters by three meters by three meters in the basement. The difficulty was to transport the earth I had thrown away out of the house, as we had to pass in front of the glazed door opening on a room usually occupied by a half a dozen Germans. Our father had a solution. He and Philip carried the earth in a small case in full view of the Germans. They never cared about what we were doing!

The hole dug, Philip fixed shelves on the four sides and our mother brought everything she would like to save from looting or destruction. This done, I built a floor over the hole and covered it with the same earth which had been used for the floor of the basement. It was so strong that no one could discover our hiding place.

Early one night our parents told us and our cousins and the maid to rush to the trench as our area was attacked. I was so tired that I was soon asleep again. In the morning our mother observed, "You slept well. Do you know what happened during your sleep?"

"I don't know," I said.

"Well," continued our mother. "Look outside."

The remains of a poor cow and a big hole were spread over the place where I had slept in the trench.

We used the trench a few more times. It was not comfortable, but we were safe inside of it. It was too dangerous to go out on the road. So we did not have any bread. It was too early to harvest potatoes. The farmers were happy to sell to us their cream, their butter, their milk, and their eggs: there was no market now to buy their goods. We were happy to get greens from the kitchen garden. From time to time we ate one of the rabbits of our mother. Our father could not get honey from his hives, as we did not have sugar to offer in exchange for the bees. This kind of diet was not too bad; it was certainly better than the one in Montreuil-sous-bois, except that we did not have our full muscular strength.

I was certainly better back at home in Hambye than in hiding. Nobody saw the French policemen. In London, some French military officers encouraged young Frenchmen to join large groups of resisters, but provided them few weapons. As they were many, it was difficult for the youth to get food, clothes, shoes, and other necessities. And as they were many, the Germans knew about them and knew how to destroy them. On the evening of June 12, German forces attacked the Maquis Prisme and killed one hundred of the resisters. Then on June 20, German artillery, tanks, and air force attacked Mont Mouchet, near Clermont-Ferrand; most of the guerillas were able to escape.

In Normandy, from June 19 to 21, strong winds destroyed one of the artificial harbors, which delayed Allied operations. But news from other parts of the world was good. The U.S. marines had landed in the Mariana Islands. The Soviets were in central Europe. The Allies had taken Rome in Italy.

The German tank which had menaced us with its gun disappeared one night. Philip had used his school German to speak with its crew. According to them, this tank was not allowed more than fifty liters of gas per day. It was not much for a vehicle of forty-five tons. They had abandoned a mysterious heavy barrel.

During a few days, we were without Germans in the house and around. We continued to be careful. They could come back at any time. It was a strange feeling of absence, like at the funeral of a bully. Something was missing; we did not wish to know. We explored the room that they had permanently occupied. They had left it empty. They had removed or destroyed everything they had and even cleaned after them.

One morning we discovered again many soldiers in green uniforms and a few in black ones around our house. The scene was strange. The men in black, some SS, were shouting to the men in green, who were moving slowly and often not at all. Again and again we heard, "Schnell!" ("Quick!").

Three of the green men, hidden from the SS by a bush of our flower garden, and who were resting, spoke to us children, "We are Czech. They have put us in an artillery unit. Our guns are ten kilometers to the south. Our shells are ten kilometers to the north. We don't have the time to get both. Next night, either we drive to the south and get our guns, but we shall be without shell; or we drive to the north, but shall not have guns for the shells."

They continued to move as slowly as they could. The SS did not stop being angry. Twenty kilometers was not a long distance for trucks. Would these Czechs be able to move so slowly that they would not be able to fight? We had observed that they had no weapons with them. The next morning, all had gone.

The presence of these Czechs, their ill will towards their SS, had given us a kind of alleviation. The bully was no longer here. There were true people around us.

On June 22, the 7th U.S. Army Corps led by General J. Lawton Collins had arrived at Cherbourg, north of the Cotentin Peninsula, and sent an ultimatum to the Germans entrenched there. Not getting an answer, General Collins started the attack the next day with the support of Allied air forces and Allied warships.

A few days earlier the slaves of the Todt Organization had been discharged towards the outskirts. Civilians were evacuated too. During a battle which lasted four days, seven ships transporting German troops tried to leave the harbor. Two of them got sunk; three others were damaged. On June 27, the Americans had conquered the city, the harbor, and the naval dockyard, but all were only ruins. It was told that a German had opened the doors of the jail, allowing the civilian prisoners—men, women, and children—to escape. The Americans had captured thirty thousand Germans, soldiers, and sailors.

In the meantime we were told that German reinforcements were on their way to Normandy, including the 2nd SS Panzer Corps, withdrawn from Russia.

The departure of the Czechs meant that we were now in a no man's land. Our parents were afraid that gangs of former Todt Organization slaves or lost German soldiers would come and plunder us, as in Coutances. One evening five soldiers of the German Army came to our door. They did not speak German, and after a while we understood that they were Ukrainians who had been recruited by the Germans. The conversation was impossible, as we had no common vocabulary. Finally they showed us a few soaps drying on the chimney mantelpiece in our kitchen, and they showed us their widely opened mouths.

"We have no food," said our mother.

We repeated, "No food," showing our stomachs and opening all our furniture, so they could see that we had no food.

At last, they showed again the soaps and requested a few of them and left.

We heard the muffled sounds of bombings far away. Most of the time, this was a machine gun we heard. Curiously, the sound of a machine gun provided some kind of security to us. Thanks to it, we knew where there were soldiers—mostly German soldiers.

The siege of Caen had started on June 7. It was difficult because Germans had fortified not only the city but also the surroundings. Many civilians were too slow to leave Caen. Hundreds of airplanes and four warships were, little by little, destroying German fortifications and, alas, killing hundreds of people and demolishing many buildings.

I was awakened one dawn by a muffled sound that did not stop. I put my shoes on and went carefully through the flower garden. Enormous shapes were rolling on the road. Hiding myself, I crawled to a bush near the fence and looked through it. I had never seen such enormous tanks. The vehicles moving in front of me were German Tigers of fifty-six tons with guns of eighty-eight millimeters. Their camouflage was in yellowish colors: our country is mostly green, and I thought that these tanks were coming from far away. They were just traveling, as the distance between them was only a few meters. Their turrets were closed, however, which meant that their crews were afraid of something. Soon it would be full daylight, and they would leave the road to hide from Allied airplanes. They were in a hurry, but tanks are relatively slow.

I felt secure behind my bush. Tanks do not see well, especially on the ground. But I felt coldness along my spine. I felt death around them. I was happy when I could get back home and again to my bed. Had the Allies the means to destroy these monsters?

General Montgomery at last decided on a frontal attack to take Caen. On July 8, Canadians and British started a difficult advance. They were opposed by sixteen- to eighteen-year-old Germans. On the July 9, the Allies had occupied the northern part of the city.

A few days later, early in the morning, we heard submachine guns around the house. Through our first floor windows we saw young German soldiers running and shooting in every direction. A cow was killed in a neighboring field. Our doors were barricaded and our windows were protected by wood shutters. As the eldest of the children, I felt a responsibility in case these Germans would enter into our house.

After a couple of hours during which we took a nervous breakfast of milk, the shooting stopped. It appeared that the youth had used all of their ammunition, but we were not ready to expose ourselves. The situation lasted for a couple of days. The Germans had even less food than us. On the third day they sat here and there and started to cry. Ernestine, a woman in her seventies, opened her door and came to them. This was exactly what they needed, the compassion of a grandmother. Ernestine did not know German; they did not know the language of Ernestine. They just needed to cry and to be patted. In the afternoon they went. Was it towards a surrendering?

Ernestine told us that these sixteen-year-olds had been surprised in their tanks near Caen. They were bombed by Allied airplanes. They had found difficult to get out of their tanks and leave the scene. Many members of their crews had been victims of the explosions. We congratulated Ernestine. She had been so brave.

"Oh, at my age it does not matter," she answered. These soldiers had been members of Hitler Youth. Two thousand civilians were killed in Caen.

On July 7, General Bradley told the 8th U.S. Army Corps to capture the south of Cotentin. Progressing through the bocage was difficult and dangerous. Each small field was surrounded by banks of earth and bushes, providing Germans many hiding possibilities. The hardest was to capture Saint-Lô, a city surrounded by hills and on a river. Thousands of U.S. soldiers died. Hitler was using some of his best units, the armored SS divisions Panzer Lehr and Das Reich, and the 17th SS Division. On July 22, Germans were gone, but the city and its surroundings were in ruins.

On July 27, 1944, we heard that Soviet troops had re-conquered the Ukraine. The following day we got excited, as we heard that General George Patton, who had distinguished himself with the 2nd U.S. Army Corps in North Africa, had been made the head of the U.S. Third Army. We also heard that Hitler had removed Marshal Gerd von Rundstedt from his command in Normandy for having advised him to make peace, and both the Normans and the Germans had interpreted this decision as a confirmation that Germany had lost the war. Patton had a reputation of being daring; his appointment meant to everybody that there would be soon a major U.S. offensive.

July 28 and 29, 1944, were days of great joy. Around 10 A.M. we saw a long file of Sherman tanks moving slowly westward on the road. Their turrets were opened and a number of soldiers in light brown outfits seemed to rest on their vehicles.

"The Americans!"

We rushed out of our houses and in minutes the whole family and the neighbors were saluting and complimenting the U.S. soldiers. We had waited so long for them. And now they were here. And the soldiers were pleased with our enthusiasm and started to give us candies, chewing gum, and cigarettes. A few asked for cognac. Our parents could give them some glasses of calvados.

We were standing all along the road, applauding and saluting ceaselessly. And they were showing big smiles.

An officer in a jeep told his soldiers and our small crowd to take cover. At two kilometers from us, a lonely German soldier directed his rifle toward us and began to shoot. The American soldiers were now in their closed tanks and we had taken cover on the side of the road which was not exposed. From time to time the German was shooting. The U.S. officer shot him and he fell. A few days later I walked by the body of this German, a young man who had a fiancée waiting for him. How could he have thought that with only a rifle it was possible for a single man to stop a file of tanks? Had his sacrifice any meaning, except to make cry those who loved him?

After his death, we continued showing the Americans how pleased we were to see them, and we did the same with the remainder of the file the following day.

Some soldiers were distributing other goodies. In this way I got some bags of coffee powder and a can of ration K. We ate the meat of the ration K at lunch, happy to have this food, but at the same time finding it too sweet and too salted. Our mother was very happy with her coffee; it was the first time she drank good coffee since 1940.

On the second day the crew of a certain tank made strong gestures toward us. We walked to them and discovered that the Ukrainians who had asked us for food were now incorporated into the U.S. armed forces and responsible for a Sherman tank.

Coutances, Lengronne and Saint-Denis-le-Gast were liberated also July 28. The Americans took the bridges on the Seinne, except one in Gavray, in order to make it difficult for the Germans to escape.

On the dawn of July 30, thirty German tanks and a number of German infantry attempted to escape between Saint-Denis-le-Gast, the community west of Hambye, and the sea. Seventeen Germans were killed, one hundred and fifty wounded. Fifteen kilometers away, all one hundred and twenty-five Germans who had tried to escape were killed. Germans tried in other places in vain. In the end the Americans had collected more than five hundred vehicles, many tanks and much artillery, and had taken a number of prisoners. On the July 31, the Cotentin Peninsula was in American hands. There were ruins everywhere. But we were happy. The problem was food and other necessities. More came every day, and we were finally able to get fine hair without lice, which was quite agreeable.

Without our knowing, there were still Germans in Hambye. We were told that the secretary of the city hall had been shot by a German officer when she had attempted to fix a flag above the entrance. A couple of German soldiers menaced us in our house to get food. They were equipped with large belts of the type used by workers who repair electrical lines and carried a number of grenades. We thought that they could hide themselves easily in trees during daytime. The worst happened to the Americans. They had built a shelter to spend the night near our house. In the morning it was discovered that their two sentries had been killed by a bayonet, and that grenades had killed the soldiers asleep in the shelter.

There were weapons everywhere. Philip and I had brought to our house a collection of Mauser rifles, helmets, insignias. In a field near our house we found a motorcycle with a sidecar and were very pleased that we could use them; we also found a German Panzer tank of medium size. Philip got inside and drove it all around the field. I was not aware that he had learned how to drive and operate a tank. He had made a model of a Panzer in wood, much admired.

Our father was becoming nervous with our findings and brought the Mauser rifles to city hall. One afternoon Philip and I discovered Hambye policemen, now in uniforms. They were coming to confiscate the motorcycle. They had served the Germans. Now they were serving the new French government. "Might is right." I found a pair of Russian boots; as they were too small for me, I gave them away with some regret after a few days. An American gave a new shirt to Philip, and as it was too large for him he gave it to me. Our father went to town hall and got his radio set back, but I continued for some time to listen on the galene set. The Germans had not removed their telephone line.

U.S. Infantry came some time later: two lines of soldiers walking on each side of the road. Granville was taken without fight. Germans there were happy to surrender. General Patton was conquering Brittany. On the August 9, Canadians and British troops were in control of the whole of Caen. Retreating Germans were encircled in the pocket of Falaise on August 19, thanks largely to the Poles, relieved by the Canadians after fighting alone for three days. Now the front would be on the Rhine River, along the German border, and in the harbors still defended by Germans.

The road in Hambye was alive again, full of American trucks and jeeps. The soldiers were happy with the welcome and we were happy with their presence, and with their chewing gum and cigarettes.

16

The Five Sisters

In October 1945, Philip and I were again studying at Voltaire high school in Paris. Beer and Bramnick had escaped persecutions and were among us. We shook their hands, but did not ask them any questions. We asked no questions of my new teacher of French, Latin, and Greek, Mr. Dreyfus, also a Jew. Through our attitudes we showed him respect. For all of us, the surprise was that Mr. Dreyfus and most of the teachers were younger and more vigorous.

The ones of us who had suffered more hunger were no longer among us. The distribution of a little food during our lectures had ended.

Philip's teachers and our father did not understand that Philip was a natural cabinetmaker like our grandfather and his father. Their contempt for handicraftsmen resulted in Philip repeating the same level for two years. He had to escape from the wrath of our father. At home in Montreuil-sous-bois, where the whole family was now living together, he made himself as invisible as he could.

At Voltaire high school, we were approached by fellow students trying to have us join the "Forces Françaises de l'Intérieur," (FFI) the communist guerillas.

"You have done a magnificent work when the Germans were here," I said. "You have sabotaged transportation to the point that they were moving too slowly for winning. But now Germans are gone."

"You believe so," they replied. "Look at what has happened when de Gaulle arrived in Paris. The policemen and the officials who had hunted the Jews, the gypsies, people with a darker skin, communists, and others did not get punished. They kept their jobs. And now they are hunting gypsies and communists the same."

It was true that youth in our school was afraid of the police which had served the Germans. Back in Paris in 1944, de Gaulle had been persuaded that he had to use this police in order to resist the Russians. Up to now, there had not been any purge or reeducation in a police force which had worked for the Nazis. . . .

I did not know what to say. All I had observed was that the women who had German friends and had not escaped were sheared by the crowd, and that the policemen and officials who had persecuted Jews and other people were left in peace. Something was in preparation which I did not understand. I said no to the FFI and to any other group. There were even grownups telling us that we should ally with the Germans and launch an offensive against Russia with generals like Patton. . . . How could they? Had not there been enough suffering? I preferred to enjoy my studies and the good food prepared by our mother and Mrs. Lahr. But in Paris, to avoid all the intense discussions and disputes was difficult.

They had not forgotten 1936. The Right refused that the country's wealth be increased through industry and commerce and wished to get larger shares. The Left defended what it had obtained in 1936 and saw in collectivism the remedy. Nobody understood that in America Ford considered his employees as his first customers, that good salaries were necessary to industrial production—a production of less expensive objects, all similar. They wished things to be made according to individual specifications. All wanted more, provided that others got less. What they wanted was the "Lutte des Classes," the class struggle, and the domination and exploitation of provinces.

So it was good to be in Hambye for the Easter holidays, as the cousins had also been invited. We were a happy group of youth in the house of my grandfather on my father's side.

Through the all of Europe, families were happy for the return of men, but not entirely. The former soldiers demanded authority and jobs. They did not understand that society had worked without them for years. Decisions were taken without them. Women and youth had done the work, and few of them were ready to abandon their new positions. We resented the arrogance of the soldiers, especially of those who had spent time in prisoner's camps.

On March 31, 1945, an object left in our grandfather's yard exploded. I got severely wounded. Gérard, the son of René and Germaine, hastened on his bicycle to the notary, as the notary was one of three persons who had been allowed to keep a car in Hambye. Soon Master Potier drove me to Villedieu, the only place where the hospital had not been destroyed. Soon I was brought to an operation room. An anesthetist told me, "Count until twenty."

I started. But at nine I lost consciousness. As a matter of fact, I found myself in another world. At first it was black, very black. But I prayed and prayed, asking God for my life. Then a good voice said, "It would better for you to die, as if you would continue living, you would suffer much."

I felt reassured that someone was listening to me. I could now distinguish in the dark a small sun, which seemed very good, and which was growing. I prayed more intensely for my life, asking God for his permission. At last I heard again the good voice. It said, "You will live a long time and get a family."

All of a sudden, I found myself high in the air. I could see the whole country, the city of Villedieu, the hospital, and in a room my mother and a nurse standing by my body. I was feeling extraordinarily light and free. When I wished to be on a certain spot, I was there immediately. It was wonderful.

Again all of a sudden I was back inside my body.

My mother was in my bedroom when I awoke from the coma. I opened my eyes with effort; she jumped and shouted, "He is alive!"

There was little I could do, so hurt I was. But my mother was always helping me, encouraging me, supporting me. I knew that she had lot to do and I was not used to so much attention from her. And as always she was effective.

I was not an easy patient. I was so much in pain at times that I was difficult. But in a couple of months my wounds had healed up; I could walk and do a few small things. In June I was fit enough for the exam of completion of secondary studies and I was successful. I believe that she did not attribute much value to this diploma, contrary to our father; but she shared my joy so openly that I was grateful to her.

When I was showing much pain, my brothers and sisters stood around me, their eyes wide open, full of sympathy, sad at not knowing what to do to soothe my suffering. I would like to give a big kiss to each of them for these demonstrations of love. But we had not been educated to do so.

After our mother had stopped to send food to the family and to some friends, a heavy task, came a period when everybody seemed to retire within themselves. Our grandmother was making rare afternoon visits to our mother and we barely met her. On the first of January 1946, the father of my father fell asleep for eternity. On a sunny day in the spring of 1948, back from my law courses, I opened the door of the house; my mother called and asked that I come up to the first floor.

I met a pretty, unknown little girl, very fair and with hair of a light ash blond typical of northern Germans. I greeted her and proceeded to the bathroom where I met my mother with her sister Theresa. My aunt looked a little afraid, but soon we were both happy to meet again.

My mother explained that the little girl was the daughter of Theresa. I congratulated Theresa for such a beautiful child. But again Theresa was afraid and I had the feeling that she was wondering if I was joking. So I did my best to show her how pleased I was to see her after years.

We went down to the kitchen to feed the little girl. Little by little I understood that Theresa had been raped. In consequence she left Le Havre. Her mother had anticipated that Le Havre, a major harbor, would be disputed between the Germans and the Allies. She had moved her furniture as well as the machines and the equipment of the Ateliers Doré to a repository near Paris, a safe place, she believed.

My grandmother, Theresa, and Lalen had found a farm near Dreux in 1943 and the four of them were living there.

Still on June 14, 1944, fifteen German submarines had attempted to find shelter in the harbor of Le Havre. In the evening, Allies bombers had sunk eleven of them and damaged three. Eight thousand German soldiers and three thousand German sailors were manning about two hundred and fifty bunkers in the area, which was not pleasant for the forty thousand inhabitants. The Allies had multiplied raids over Le Havre. But on June 15, they sent three hundred and fifty airplanes above the city. Civilian casualties increased. But the Allies did not stop. On September 4, General John Crocker of the First British Corps, forty-five thousand men strong, sent an ultimatum. On the following day Colonel Eberhard Wildermuth rejected its terms, a decision which cost dearly the city and its inhabitants. During the week starting on September 5, four hundred naval guns and more planes than before destroyed the center, killing three thousand civilians. On September 10, the British and some FFI started the assault. In the evening of the

September 12, the city was theirs. Its center was completely demolished. My grandmother and her children were never able to locate Francis the First Boulevard.

Right after the war, priority had been given to reconstruct railway tracks and industries of use for rebuilding in general. The decision had been made to make Le Havre a new city. It postponed rebuilding. Our grandmother often spoke with the planners of Le Havre, and also with those of Caen and Rouen where the Ateliers Doré were active before the war. No one disputed the usefulness of her enterprise, not only to help to the reconstruction but also to start again the activities linked to the harbor and which provided foreign currencies. At last she got three large plots and the authorization for building. It did not take very long to have the machinery back. The problem was to house the personnel. There were very few houses.

As the work of our father was getting recognition: his pay increased. Our family moved to a large apartment in Paris, but I was already at the "Cité Internationale universitaire" where students from the whole world were learning to respect, appreciate, and even like people of all countries. Our mother invited Gabrielle, Taee, Vev, and Theresa as well as other family to a party in her new apartment. I was so joyful to meet again my four aunts. Much had happened to each of them. Taee and Vev had worked for the Red Cross, which gave each of them the opportunity to get a husband. During the time of the Germans, Taee had also helped *Combat*, a resistance newspaper. She was carrying paper for it. The leaves were very small. But paper is heavy. She was traveling by using the subway, and every time there was a German control she used her fair hair, her blue eyes, and a big smile. They never stopped her.

The little daughter of Theresa was a curious person and one day drank a bottle of eau de cologne. It had not been possible to save her life at the hospital. Theresa was a typist, speaking two languages. And Gabrielle was a typist too.

Our grandmother was at last able to invite Philip and me to visit her in Le Havre. It was in 1954. She had not found a large house to compensate for her loss, but two apartments where she had brought back part of her furniture. The arrival at the railway station had been without any surprise. It had not been destroyed and remained as in our memories. But everything was new in the area our grandmother was living. We were pleased to see her again, with her way of not looking important and her few sentences. She did look the same to us, but she had been through difficult years. There was no work at the time of the German colonization, so many expenses for her and for the Ateliers had been financed by a bank. When the Ateliers started to work again, they earned some money and my grandmother could start to repay the bank. But the government decided that its payments would no longer be as usual, but in treasury bonds. At the beginning, the bank accepted the treasury bonds, but soon discovered that it could not get money for them. The bank could therefore no longer accept the treasury bonds from its customers. Our grandmother took then the decision to sell her castle in Les Hellandes, which allowed her to reimburse much of her debts to the bank. She also decided that as long as the customers would like to pay in treasury bonds, the Ateliers Doré would be slow at delivery.

Our grandmother had received, however, a splendid gift in one of her apartment: a very large window opening on the harbor and the sea. Everybody spent time looking through it. Philip and I walked to the Sugar Loaf, which had remained intact as well as the little chapel by it. We were still able to walk on the pier. Much of our walking was exploratory, as everything had been changed. Now along the sea was a large sandy beach developed on the rubbish of the city pushed by bulldozers, where people had fun without thinking about what was under their feet.

My grandmother died in 1956. My aunts had been around her. I had arrived too late. It was a great loss. She had visited my parents' family several times. She had suffered more and more; doctors at this time did not know how to cure a colon cancer, a hereditary sickness in our family. She had also visited several times each of her other children, save Lalen who was still living with her. She had known their families and got pleasure from them.

Later, I also kept visiting my parents and my aunts. I liked the husbands of Taee, Vev, and Theresa and was sorry for my poor aunt Gabrielle who had married an egoist. I continued for years to have the love of five mothers, the five sisters: my aunts, and my mother.

It looked like rain. The Le Regent theater offered a movie about the Battle of the Midway Islands. I had enough money for a seat.

In the darkness of the room, I saw in color—I was used to black and white movies—a beautiful sky and a beautiful sea, and the most formidable warships I had ever imagined. The spectacle was accompanied by a music I was not used to. At enormous distances, a Japanese fleet was deployed on the huge ocean to try vainly to stop the American navy.

Suddenly I started to shake. I could not stop it. My all body was shaking. This lasted until I had watched the whole movie and continued on the street, under the rain. Only walking back home took care little by little of my body. War had never made me afraid before watching this movie. Airplanes in the sky, noises in the night, even silences made me afraid for years. But that is the past today.

Francis the 1st Boulevard in Le Havre in the late forties. *Edition CM, Le Havre.*

The Havel family house in La Cave, Hambye (center and left of the photograph). To the left, there is a new farm building. A fire had destroyed the old one. The administration ordered our father not to rebuild it. But the farmer had no place for his hay. Our father rebuilt the building. The administration ordered him to demolish it! A judge, supported by the local people, took the side of our father. This was in the late forties. The photograph is from 1957.

CPSIA information can be obtained at www.ICGtesting.com
Printed in the USA
LVOW042132190912
299489LV00001B/1/P